Teaching a

An alterna
to teaching an

Kieran Egan

Routledge

First published in 1988 by
Routledge
11 New Fetter Lane, London EC4P 4EE
Reprinted 1990

Printed in Great Britain by
T.J. Press (Padstow) Ltd, Padstow, Cornwall

British Library Cataloguing in Publication Data
Egan, Kieran
    Teaching as story telling: an alternative approach to
    teaching and the curriculum.
    1. Schools. Teaching methods
    I. Title
    371.3

ISBN 0-415-00700-3

CONTENTS

ACKNOWLEDGEMENTS

I am grateful for the helpful comments made by many kind people on the ms. of this book. A number of teachers at Westwind School in Richmond, British Columbia have been most generous with their time, insightful criticism, and practical wisdom; my thanks to June Chiba, Barbara Gawa, Merrilee Prentice, Janet White, and Craig Worthing, and most of all to Sandy Oldfield, who has questioned, encouraged, prodded me and tried out and adapted this model a number of ways. An assignment of my Education 911 course in the Fall of 1984 was the production of a publishable work. This was mine, composed through a barrage of criticism, abuse, and most helpful comments from Pirie Mitchell, Rob Wood, Wendy Strachan, and Lee Dobson. The ms. has been improved also as a result of the suggestions of colleagues at Simon Fraser University. Among those who kindly read the ms. or parts of it are Cornel Hamm, Dan Nadaner, Suzanne de Castell, Meguido Zola, Selma Wasserman, Tom O'Shea, Jaap Tuinman, Robin Barrow, Dennis Smith, and Ian Andrews. I am most grateful for their generously given criticisms. I have benefited also from discussions with members of the staff of Wesley College, Melbourne, in particular Di Fleming and Tony Conabere. Alan Gregory and Peter Musgrave of Monash University both read the ms. and have given useful criticisms. Elaine McKay, John Shelton, Ida and Hugo McCann and Mike Degenhardt of the University of

Tasmania have helped me to reflect on and reconsider various parts of the argument. Maxine Greene's (Teachers College, Columbia University) criticisms of the article on which Chapter One is based have been most stimulating. Susanna Egan has improved the ms. with her usual range of insightful comments and editorial advice. It is a pleasure to thank Eileen Mallory for typing the ms., or "processing" it, with unfailing cheerfulness and impossible speed and efficiency.

Two parts of this book have appeared in journal articles. Some of Chapter One appeared in "Imagination and Learning," *Teachers College Record*, Winter, 1985, and a few sections from Chapter Three appeared in "Teaching as Story Telling," *Journal of Curriculum Studies*, October-December, 1985. I am grateful to the editors and publishers of these journals for permission to reprint these sections here.

INTRODUCTION

This book is offered as an alternative approach to planning teaching. An alternative to what, and what kind of alternative? It is an alternative to the dominant procedure recommended for planning lessons and units of study, and an alternative to some of the dominant principles recommended for selecting content for teaching. In nearly all teacher preparation programs students are taught that in planning lessons and units they should first identify and list their objectives, then select content and materials, then choose appropriate methods, and then decide on evaluation procedures. Students are also taught as guiding principles that children's learning proceeds from the concrete to the abstract, from the known to the unknown, from the simple to the complex, and from active manipulation to symbolic conceptualization.

My first task will be to try to show that we do need alternatives to this model and these principles. I will argue that the objectives—content—methods—evaluation model can lead to an inappropriately mechanistic way of thinking about planning teaching. Similarly, I will try to show that the principles about children's learning are at best inadequate, and lead us largely to ignore the most powerful tools for learning that children bring with them to school. The dominant model and principles are derived from educational research and theorizing that has almost entirely ignored the power and educational uses of children's imagination.

1

A continuing theme of this book is that children's imaginations are the most powerful and energetic learning tools. Our most influential learning theories have been formed from research programs that have very largely focused on a limited range of children's logical thinking skills. That research has largely neglected imagination, because imagination is, after all, difficult stuff to get any clear hold on. Consequently the dominant learning theories that have profoundly influenced education, helping to form the dominant model and principles mentioned above, have taken little account of imagination. A constant focus of this book, then, will be on areas of children's intellectual activity in which we can see imagination at work, or play. Especially I will focus on children's stories, particularly fantasy stories. By keeping imaginative intellectual activity to the fore I will try to redress an imbalance in our general view of the child as a learner.

What kind of alternative is offered here? It is a model for planning teaching that encourages us to see lessons or units as good stories to be told rather than sets of objectives to be attained. It is an organic approach that puts *meaning* center-stage. It is an approach that draws on more adequate principles of learning; principles that use and stimulate children's imagination. This book is built around a new planning model for teaching; a model primarily concerned with providing children with access to and engagement with rich meaning.

This is not a book about how to teach using fictional stories, nor is it about how to tell stories effectively. Rather it is about how to use the power of the story form in order to teach any content more engagingly and meaningfully.

The story form is a cultural universal; everyone everywhere enjoys stories. The story, then, is not just some casual entertainment; it reflects a basic and powerful form in which we make sense of the world and experience. Indeed some people claim that the story form reflects a fundamental structure of our minds (Lévi-Strauss, 1966). Whatever the case, it is clear that children are readily and powerfully engaged by stories. This book is an attempt to design a model that draws on the power of the story form and uses that power in teaching.

I will describe the model in detail and give a number of examples of its use in different curriculum areas. Because it conflicts at a number of points with some of the presently dominant principles and procedures, it seems best to begin by discussing those principles and procedures.

In the first chapter, then, I will consider such prominent principles as "from the concrete to the abstract" and "from the known to the unknown." Few people take these as universally true, of course, but I will try to show how such principles are enormously influential, sometimes in subtle ways. Also I will try to show how that influence can be educationally destructive. My main concern will be to show that these are principles of learning that have been formulated very largely with no reference to children's imagination. By considering children's imagination, particularly as it is evident in fantasy stories, we can see clearly some of the inadequacies of these principles, and can formulate for ourselves more adequate and practical principles.

Because the model draws primarily on the story form, I will discuss stories in detail, in the second chapter. As an introduction to the model I will describe some of the elements of stories. I will focus on just a few such elements; those that are crucial to the power of stories to engage children. With these in mind, the inadequacies of the objectives—content—methods—evaluation model will be examined.

In the third chapter I will present my alternative model for planning teaching. The basic model is quite compact, designed, following the example of Ralph Tyler (1949), as a set of questions, the answers to which will provide a lesson or unit plan. The purpose is to shape the lesson or unit to use the engaging power of the story form and to ensure that the most important meanings inherent in the content are communicated. I will show the way the model can be used in planning a unit on Communities and a lesson on the Vikings.

The fourth chapter will be taken up with various additional examples of using the model in a variety of curriculum areas. We tend to assume that the story form can deal only with events, but I will try to show how it can also shape the teaching of mathematics and science to fulfill the aim of meaningful teaching.

In the final chapter I will discuss some implications of the alternative principles I propose for the curriculum. One cannot, of course, separate teaching and curriculum in any radical way. Attempts to dispute principles used in selecting content for particular lessons and units will necessarily have some impact on the overall selection and sequencing of content in the curriculum. I will make a case for considerably enriching the content of the elementary school curriculum, in order to provide children with things to think about that challenge and stimulate the imaginative powers they think with.

CHAPTER 1

Imagination and Learning

Because imagination is difficult to get any firm grasp on, there has been little educational research which focuses on it. Most educational research has difficulty enough dealing with things like knowledge, learning, or development. These are things our methods of research seem able to get some kind of hold on. So we have a great deal of research on the more easily grasped stuff and very little on imagination.

Unfortunately, what we focus on tends to take a disproportionate space in our field of vision. If you were to try to draw from memory a proportionate picture of the moon, you would likely find on comparing it with reality that you had drawn your moon much too big. It is, after all, what we usually focus on in our casual looks up at the night sky. Similarly, what we study within the broad realm of education tends to be disproportionately influential on our thinking about educational practice.

Everyone acknowledges the importance of imagination in education. But we do not have large and energetic programs of research focused on imagination which are constantly feeding their findings and implications into educational practice. We do see such influences on practice from educational psychology, philosophy, sociology and so on, in all of which imagination is largely ignored.

Each individual teacher and curriculum designer tends not to be excessively influenced by particular research studies or theories, of course. We compose our views gradually and eclectically from a wide range of theories and research findings in light of our own experiences. From these we tend to form what I may perhaps call "*ad hoc* principles" which guide our teaching or curriculum choices. If research and theories contribute to these *ad hoc* principles, and this research and these theories tend to ignore imagination, we may expect to find these principles seriously deficient. My purpose in this chapter is to argue that some of the most influential principles presently in vogue about teaching and curricula tend to suppress children's imagination and undermine some of its potential educational uses.

Let me take a few such *ad hoc* principles. I choose this set because they are enormously influential and I am sure every teacher has heard them in one form or another, and also because I suspect most teachers and other educators accept them as providing useful guidance. Educational development proceeds, these principles inform us, from the concrete to the abstract, from the simple to the complex, from the known to the unknown, from active manipulation to symbolic conceptualization. These *ad hoc* principles are not, of course, usually taken as universally true. (Language learning is a complex, abstract task mastered very early; certain simple insights come only after long study.) But I think it is fair to say that these *ad hoc* principles have a pervasive and profound influence on teaching practice and on curriculum design.

Most teachers of young children learn in their professional preparation that children's active manipulation of concrete objects should precede abstract or symbolic learning. It is a commonplace of such programs that in planning teaching we should begin with familiar knowledge and experiences and expand gradually towards new material. These principles are also powerfully influential in shaping the elementary school curriculum. They are most clearly evident in social studies; we begin with the child and present concrete experiences, then focus on the family, then on to communities, working gradually outwards to the broader society and culture realms of the world. A metaphor for this process, influential in the early formulation of the social studies curriculum, was the concentric circles of the spider's web, along the rays of which the child could expand to increasingly distant circles from the home starting point (Dodge and Kirchwey, 1901, p 69).

And what role does imagination play in shaping these *ad hoc* principles? Well, what *is* imagination? According to a standard dictionary definition it is "the act or power of forming mental images of what is not actually present," or "the act or power of creating mental images of what has never been actually experienced."

Imagination seems to have had no influence at all on the *ad hoc* principles. The sense of the child as an energetic creator of mental images of what may never have been experienced seems, on the face of it at least, to conflict with the sense of the child presented in the *ad hoc* principles that have been so influential in education. Is the child who manipulates concrete materials derived from everyday experience the same child whose mind is brimming with star-warriors, monsters, and wicked witches? And is it more or less important for future educational development that a child be able to create and mentally manipulate these imaginary creatures than that the child be able to conserve liquid volume?

I will look at some of these *ad hoc* principles, then, in the light of some kinds of intellectual activity in which we can see imagination energetically at work. I will begin by considering how just a few features of young children's fantasy might influence or challenge these principles.

FROM THE CONCRETE TO THE ABSTRACT

I have suggested that there is an apparent conflict between the images of the child that emerge from the *ad hoc* principles on the one hand and from our common observations of children's imaginativeness on the other. Let us consider whether this conflict isn't more than merely apparent. If we accept the principle that children's learning progresses from the concrete to the abstract, for example, how do we deal with fantasy stories?

In education this *ad hoc* principle is used quite widely, to support both the claim that we should begin teaching with concrete *material* things and move from these towards abstract concepts, and also that in learning any subject we should work from particulars within the experience of the child in the direction of greater abstraction. We commonly hear confidently asserted such claims as "Children learn best from concrete, hands-on experiences." We need to ask whether children learn *everything* best from such experiences. Can they learn *only* from such experiences? Are there things that *cannot* be learned from such experiences? Are there things that are best learned from other kinds of experiences? And so on.

If we take a story such as *Cinderella*, which seems to cause few comprehension problems for the average five year old, or those jolly narratives in which Mr. Worm and Mrs. Butterfly chat casually about the weather as they go about their various middle-class tasks of shopping or gardening, it is clear that such stories are structured on the relationship of various underlying concepts. In the case of *Cinderella*, we can immediately see conflicts of fear/hope, kindness/cruelty, and, of course, good/bad. These are enormously general, abstract concepts. There is an obvious sense in which children must "have" these abstract concepts for the "concrete" story of Cinderella to make sense. That is, the abstraction is prior and prerequisite to being able to understand the concrete story.

An immediate objection to this conclusion is that the abstract concepts — fear/hope, good/bad — have been generated from earlier concrete experiences. I will return to this below.

Another apparent counter-example to the *ad hoc* principle will be evident to anyone who has read a book like *The Lord of the Rings* to a child. The parts of the narrative that are most comprehensible and engaging are those whose meaning turns on the child's understanding of abstract concepts like loyalty/betrayal, courage/cowardice, honor/selfishness. Without such concepts most of the concrete action in the book is meaningless. Such concepts are not generated by the actions; the abstract concepts have to be already understood for the actions to make sense. Those parts of the narrative that are least engaging and comprehensive are indeed "concrete" descriptions of landscape, weather, flora, and so on. Now obviously we can provide explanations of such observations; their point here is only that they seem to conflict with the principle that children's understanding proceeds from the concrete to the abstract.

It has been argued that we do not — cannot — infer grammar from the scattered examples of speech that we hear. Similarly, and perhaps more obviously, we do not infer plot forms from hearing a few particular concrete stories. Stories make sense as stories only if we already have some abstract notion of plot to organize and make meaningful the affective force of the story. Very young children, for example, know that the satisfaction of certain expectations, set up in the beginning, signals the end of the story. The abstract underlying plot-rhythm of expectation and satisfaction, then, precedes and is prerequisite to stories being meaningful.

Here, then, are three examples which — superficially at least — seem to conflict with the *ad hoc* principle that we proceed from the concrete to the abstract. Nor are they trivial or arcane matters. Indeed the centrality of these abstract organizing tools that young children deploy so readily making sense of all kinds of things may make us wonder whether the *ad hoc* principle hasn't got matters entirely the wrong way round, and that children's educational development should proceed from the abstract to the concrete.

Well, we would obviously be unwise to try to swing to the opposite extreme. The plausibility of the *ad hoc* principle depends on its being able to reflect something about how we learn various kinds of skills. We come to understand chess by learning the particular, concrete, moves of each piece and then putting these together till we achieve an abstract understanding of the rules that govern the game. (Though even here, of course, one might want to say that some general notion of the intent of the game has to precede making sense of the individual piece's moves.) Also in mastering a language — and this is perhaps the most persuasive support for the principle — more concrete terms precede abstract terms. Children seem to use more concrete terms more readily and easily and often have difficulty with abstract terms.

From such support the *ad hoc* principle may move to a counter-attack against my observations from children's fantasy stories. It might be argued that our ability to understand *Cinderella* or *The Lord of the Rings* comes from prior concrete experience having generated the abstract concepts required for comprehension of the story. And even grasp of plot-forms comes from prior concrete experiences, such as the rhythm of expectation and satisfaction that the baby knows in getting hungry and being fed.

Now it will perhaps be obvious that this argument can merrily chug along for some time. The problems with where it is chugging us to are, at least, two-fold. First, it is moving us increasingly far from the way the *ad hoc* principle is understood and put into practice in education. In education it is used to support, for example, beginning mathematics teaching with blocks or fruit-pips, and with organizing the social studies curriculum so that families and neighbourhoods precede history. And second, it is taking us into one of the most complex and contentious of philosophical questions; one that has been intensely debated from the time of the ancient Greeks — that particulars and abstractions seem to presuppose each other.

I will not resolve this philosophical question here, or anywhere. But I can think of no way of avoiding it. To challenge the *ad hoc* principle, then, requires that I at least indicate that its counter-attack against my earlier examples is itself not immune from attack. The counter-attack is that all abstractions that we see young children using are themselves the product of prior concrete experiences.

Before my counter-counter-attack I should perhaps stress that as far as educational uses of the principle are concerned the earlier observations carry some weight. The principle has been used gradually to leach out of the curriculum and teaching practice a reliance upon or use of abstract concepts. The irrefutable point made by the examples of children's fantasy is that even though young children might not articulate abstract terms and have difficulty with *certain kinds* of abstract concepts, it is not true that abstract concepts in general are difficult for young children. Indeed we see children constantly use flexibly and easily the most abstract concepts, such as good/bad. So while the *ad hoc* principle is supported by certain learning processes in young children, it is not valid for all kinds of things that young children can do. It is, in its usual educational interpretation, appropriate only in some respects some of the time, and when taken as generally valid that is the beginnings of serious imbalance and educational problems.

A medieval equivalent of *Coles Notes* summed up Aristotle's view of how we acquire knowledge as: *nihil in intellectu quod non prius in sensu.* (There is nothing in the mind except what has passed through the senses.) In this view, knowledge, however abstract, is achieved only from concrete particulars. In a more modern formulation we find it encapsulated in William James's plausible, indeed imaginative, picture of the baby experiencing a "blooming, buzzing confusion," out of which and from the particulars of which we gradually induce abstract concepts.

The conflicting, anti-empiricist or neo-rationalist, view is that we arrive in the world with minds structured in particular ways and predisposed to recognize certain patterns and make sense of the world and experience in certain ways. The baby, in this view, experiences a structured world in which certain particulars gradually become distinct as they can be fitted to the mental structures that we are born with. Knowledge is thus composed not merely by experience, but the mind constructively makes its own contribution. In this view, all our knowledge and all our actions are governed by abstract rules, which we "have" and use even though we are not necessarily conscious of them.

The philosophical and psychological support for this view is considerable, and becoming dominant it seems fair to say. But my point here is not to amass the arguments in favor of it, so much as to indicate that the counter-attack made by the *ad hoc* principle is hardly itself unassailable.

I am not trying to establish the primacy of the abstract in children's learning (for such an argument see Hayek, 1969), but only trying to counter the claim for the primacy of the concrete. What can most sensibly be concluded about human learning at present is that the phenomena are vastly more complex that any of our psychological models or the *ad hoc* principles educators derive from them. We can also sensibly question the *adequacy* of the *ad hoc* principle for the educational uses it is made to serve, and consequently question the educational adequacy of those practices and curricula based on the principle. Influenced by this principle, the experience of young children in elementary school classrooms is predominantly involved with the simple and the concrete. There is an avoidance of abstraction because the *ad hoc* principle has persuaded teachers and curriculum developers that abstract concepts are beyond the comprehension of young children. At the simplest level we may say that there is a confusion between children's ability to articulate abstractions and their ability to use them. It may be that typical five-year-olds could not adequately define loyalty or courage, but they use such concepts clearly in making sense of all kinds of stories. There is a sense in which we might say that children understand such concepts so profoundly that they understand *with* them: they use them to make sense of new knowledge.

I think it is fair to conclude that seeing the process of education as a development from the concrete to the abstract is a result of focusing on certain limited logical intellectual activities. But if we make vivid imaginative intellectual activity the focus of our attention, the general adequacy of the *ad hoc* principle is brought into question. It is at best a partial truth, but also a partial falsehood. As such we would likely be better off abandoning it and looking for a more adequate *ad hoc* principle. Of course children have difficulty learning some things, but we should give up accepting as an adequate explanation of those difficulties, that there is inherent in children's intellectual development a progression from the concrete to the abstract.

FROM THE KNOWN TO THE UNKNOWN

What about the related *ad hoc* principle about moving from the known to the unknown? If this is true, how can we explain children's easy engagement with star-warriors, wicked-witches, and talking middle-class worms? We are not here looking for a psychological or psychoanalytic explanation. We could line up the competing arguments about why such creatures are so prominent in young children's mental lives, but these explanations do not help us with the educational claim that children's learning progresses gradually "outward" from present, local experience to the unknown.

This *ad hoc* principle, again, is not some trivial or arcane matter in education; it is enormously influential. Along with the previous principle, it offers about the only organizing element to the curriculum jumble called social studies, and it is prominently invoked in designing lessons and units of study at all levels of schooling.

By considering the content of young children's fantasy stories and their own imaginative games we are surely forced to wonder about the general adequacy of a principle that claims that our knowledge of the world and experience accumulates gradually from the known to the unknown. Are wicked-witches and talking middle-class worms so prominent a part of the known world of children? Well, in one sense of course we must say yes. Such figures are all around them in books and on T.V. But this only moves the problem to a different context. Why are such fantastic creatures so engaging to young children? It is not enough to conclude simply that such creatures are foisted on children by grown-ups. They fill the world's myth-stories and haunt our dreams. They represent something about the vivid imaginative creativity of the human mind.

If we view children's education in terms of the progressive mastery of practical tasks and logical sequences of discipline areas then we can reasonably invoke the known-to-unknown principle. It will guide us to begin with children's present experiences and move gradually outward along lines of content associations. This principle indeed does shape our curricula, and we are no doubt all familiar with charts that gradually plod outward in such logical sequences from what is assumed to be the contents of children's experience.

Whatever the organizing value of this principle, we surely recognize — without having to analyse children's fantasy — that it inadequately describes our own educational development. Consider how you learned whatever you consider most valuable. We pick up bits and pieces, and suddenly see connections; these break or defract, and are recomposed in new ways with disparate pieces.

If we consider briefly children's fantasy stories, and

recall the objections to the previous principle, we can surely recognize that we directly make sense of all kinds of new knowledge by fitting it to our abstract schemes. Frodo's journey to Mordor *makes sense* (even before we consider the story's affective power) because we can fit all the new elements and events to our abstract categories of good/bad, courage/cowardice, honor/greed, and so on. That is, we see in such simple cases that we can readily understand all kinds of new material by a principle that does not at all require us to move outward along lines of content associations, connecting new knowledge to that which the child already has. We can introduce any knowledge as long as we ensure that it fits the abstract conceptual structures the child has in place.

History, then, need not remain untouched in the primary school, its absence at present being justified on the grounds that children lack the abstract concepts that are necessary to make history meaningful: chronological time, causality, and so on. From observing how children make sense of fantasy stories, we can see that they do have available conceptual tools that can make history meaningful. They may lack a logical conception of causality, but they clearly have available the sense of causality that holds stories together and moves them along: the conceptual tools that can make sense of *Cinderella* and *Lord of the Rings* can be used to make sense of the Athenians' struggle for freedom against the tyrannous Persian Empire, or the monks' struggle to preserve civilized learning against the ravages of the Vikings. Nor need such understanding of history be trivial. Young children have the conceptual tools to learn the most profound things about our past; as a struggle for freedom against arbitrary violence, for security against fear, for knowledge against ignorance, and so on. *They do not learn those concepts; they already have them when they arrive at school. They use those concepts to learn about the world and experience.*

Now we might want to engage in all kinds of arguments about the educational value of such history at the beginning of children's schooling: The only point I am making here is that the known-to-unknown principle is an inadequate guide to what children can learn.

If we consider a little further how we progressively apply our abstract organizing categories to making fuller sense of experience, we might even further reject the known-to-unknown principle. One common procedure we see at work in children's learning is the dialectical process of forming binary opposites and mediating between them. For example, in learning the temperature continuum, children tend first to learn the binary opposite concepts of "hot" and "cold." Next they mediate between these and learn the concept "warm." This is elaborated by then mediating between, say, "warm" and "cold," and the concept of "cool" or "fairly cold" is established. Some people claim this is a fundamental structure of all human learning (Lévi-Strauss, 1966; and neo-Hegelians of all kinds). We need accept this no more than we need accept the known to unknown principle. What we can commonly observe, however, are examples of this binary opposite formation and mediation at work. Also it is a model that conflicts with the *ad hoc* principle that determines so much educational practice.

Just in passing, and ignoring my earlier claim that we would be unconcerned with explanations, we might consider the pervasiveness of this binary opposites and mediation process. It seems to be one of the mind's commoner procedures for trying to make sense of the world and experience. It suggests interesting explanations for much of the fantastic content of children's thinking. If you look at the world through the eyes of a child, and you use the reliable dialectical process that is helping to make sense of much of what you see, then you will note what seems like an empirically sound binary distinction between nature and culture. If you are a child you will not likely put it in these terms, of course, but you will notice that however much you talk to the cat, it won't talk back, and however much you encourage them, the guinea pig and the gerbil will not make clothes for themselves nor tables and chairs for their cage. If you try to use the mediating process that has done you so well in being able to make sense of and talk about continua of temperature, and speed, size, and much else, you will search for categories that mediate between nature and culture. If you cannot find them, that mental process will create them. So you will generate things like talking middle-class worms. Such a creature is a mediation between nature and culture, as warm is a mediation between hot and cold. Similarly, you will observe a binary distinction between life and death. You will mediate and create ghosts, spirits, and all kinds of beings which are both alive and dead, as warm is hot and cold and middle-class worms are natural and cultural. My point here is only that this particular process of learning seems to be derived from the way the mind is programmed to learn, and proceeds even in the face of empirical reality, generating mediations which require imaginative creation. The logical plodding known-to-unknown principle does not account for this most powerful tool.

Now it might be argued that the known-to-unknown principle *does* account for this and any other counter-examples. It might be claimed that in the case of the abstract categories which allow us to make sense of any new content organized on them, that the abstract categories are "the known" and we use them to make sense of the "unknown" content. And in the previous example, it may be claimed that the binary opposites are "the known" and we mediate from them to an "unknown." Certainly this interpretation saves the principle. And the value of the principle may be reinterpreted as pointing up that we need to be sure that new content can be structured on "known" abstract categories, or that it be a mediation between "known" binary opposites. Its purpose remains to remind us that there needs to be some coherence in the sequencing of children's learning.

We *can* save the principle this way, but two points need to be made. First, it is saved by widening its interpretation to the point of making it a rather vacuous truism. Second, its interpretation so far has been used to support a curriculum and teaching practices based on expanding content associations. By focusing briefly on children's imaginative activities, we see that learning can expand a number of different ways, and that some of them seem much more pervasive and powerful than that captured in the known-to-unknown principle. The principle has been an instrument of highlighting one process of learning at the expense of others; especially at the expense of those associated with the use of imagination. Of course there are senses in which the *ad hoc* principle represents some truth, but it has falsified more than it has clarified. Its acceptance as generally true is to see the whole night sky filled with moon.

CONCLUSION

The remaining principles I mentioned above — from the simple to the complex and from active manipulation to symbolic conceptualization — are clearly related to the two I have discussed. Given more space, those too could be discussed in detail, and we could also consider the history of these principles. They are all principles that have emerged from viewing the child as a prosaic thinker with not well developed capacities for dealing with certain logical and technical tasks.

They are principles that can survive only by ignoring the highly developed imaginative capacities of children and the immensely energetic forms of learning that they clearly use constantly and which can be seen more readily if we focus on imaginative activities. Teaching practices and curricula that are derived from research which views the child's imagination as largely irrelevant to learning are not calculated either to use or to develop the imaginative capacities of children.

My point is not that we should increase the fantasy content of school curricula. Others adequately make the case for the use of the arts in general as stimulants of these capacities. My point is that we need, for the educational benefit of children, to reconstruct our curricula and teaching methods in light of a richer image of the child as an imaginative as well as a logico-mathematical thinker. What we call imagination is also a tool of learning — in the early years perhaps the most energetic and powerful one. The influence of the *ad hoc* principles I have been discussing has been to produce a curriculum and teaching methods that have excluded much of the richness of human experience to which young children can have direct access. They do this because such rich intellectual experience cannot be fitted to their arid and impoverished image of the child. What cannot be made concretely manipulable and directly tied to some simple content within the child's immediate experience has been increasingly forced out of the early school curriculum. We are treating young children as fools. Our early childhood curricula and practices are largely filled with trivia — except where the imaginative work of individual teachers counters the influence of these principles. The most powerful and energetic intellectual tools children bring to school are largely ignored and excluded when research is conducted on children's learning, intelligence, development, and so on. The products of that research then seep into education and support the kinds of *ad hoc* principles considered above. And these have been powerfully if subtlely influential in shaping curricula and in forming teachers' preconceptions about what and how children can best learn.

Perhaps ironically my conclusion from a focus on children's fantasy is that a more academically rich curriculum is appropriate in the early years. Children's imaginative capacities, let me stress, do not only find an outlet in fantasy stories: they find their real work and growth in being applied to history, mathematics, and the sciences as well.

An impoverished empiricist view of science has misused the authority of science to promote in education a narrow kind of logical thinking at the expense of those forms of thinking which we see most clearly in children's imaginative activities. The prevalence of this view has served to push imagination to the educational "sidelines" — to the "frills" of art, music, and so on, from which it can less easily be displaced. As this essentially nineteenth-century view of science finally recedes, and a more balanced view of science as a human activity becomes dominant, we in education might sensibly try to establish a more balanced view of children's thinking and learning. The *ad hoc* principles I have discussed are the remnants of the old unbalanced view. My purpose in this chapter has been to argue that imagination is a powerful and neglected tool of learning, and that we need to rethink our teaching practices and curricula with a more balanced appreciation of children's intellectual capacities. Prominent among those intellectual capacities is imagination. By ridding ourselves of the influential and restrictive *ad hoc* principles, we can see our way to enormously enriching the elementary school. We can provide children with things to think about that challenge and stimulate the imaginative powers they have to think with.

CHAPTER 2

Stories, Metaphors and Objectives

INTRODUCTION

The critical comments about educational research in the previous chapter are meant as a caution against over generalizing from limited principles and from particular, limited results. No doubt most researchers are aware of the limits of their methods, but it is natural to try to stretch inferences from results as far as possible. We need whatever help we can get, and research on learning, development, motivation, etc., seems to offer some, if often opaque, guidance. The problem I am mainly concerned with here is the imbalance in our image of the child that results from focusing very largely on a limited range of thinking skills.

The problem, I have suggested, is exacerbated by our focus having been directed by the dominant forms of research on those skills children are least good at. If, instead of focusing on the development of logico-mathematical capacities, we were to focus on the development of imaginative capacities, we would no doubt produce a quite different profile of intellectual development. Indeed, the main result I suspect would be to point up similarities between children's and adult thinking. Piaget's influential focus on children's logico-mathematical thinking has pointed up the area where the difference between children's and adult thinking are most pronounced. Piaget's work has as a result, perhaps surprisingly, been most influential in education in a restrictive way. That is, most of the inferences one sees in education from his learn-ing/development theory concern what children cannot do.

Some people might no doubt want to point out that Piaget has derived his theory from a study of play, dreams, and many other aspects of children's activity that are centrally concerned with imagination. The subject matter of his re-search has indeed included such material, but the aim has not been to study fantasy and imagination so much as to un-cover from children's responses the logico-mathematical forms that underlie them. The free, imaginative content is typically given short shrift: "One would like to be able to rule out romancing with the same severity as (those answers designed to please the questioner)" (Piaget, 1951, p. 10). Similarly, most research on children's story comprehension misses their imaginative qualities and focuses on the familiar range of "graspable" logical skills (see, e.g., Stein and Trabasso, 1981).

If we continue to keep imaginative intellectual activity as our focus we might be able to construct a more hopeful and less constrictive image of the child as learner. Such an image would, it seems to me, be more in keeping with our everyday experience of children's creative intellectual energy than is the Piagetian view of relative intellectual incompetents. This is not to say that we will now ignore what children typically seem unable to do, but rather that we will focus on what they most obviously *can* do, and seem able to do best.

In the previous chapter, for example, it was noted that some Piagetian research suggests that children do not typical-ly in elementary school years "develop" a concept of historical causality (Hallam, 1966, 1975). We can observe, however, that children clearly have available a concept of the kind of causality that keeps stories together and moves them along. Such a simple observation has an obvious educational implication. It is clearly insufficient to do a research study that concludes that "causality" is a "formal operational" con-cept, in Piaget's sense, and that young children thus cannot understand or use it, and then infer further that curriculum content requiring or using this concept should be excluded from the elementary school curriculum. Yet this very com-monly is the kind of "educational implication" derived from

Piaget's theory. Thus we see recommendations that in elementary schools we should always deal with experiences which "emphasise *direct* contact with the physical aspects of objects and events" (Wadsworth, 1978, p. 186).

There are two educational problems with such common "Piagetian" recommendations. First, the theme of the previous chapter, they take logico-mathematical thinking as the whole of thinking, (their night sky is nothing but Piagetian moon). Second, they neglect the early stimulation and development of those concepts out of which the more formal logico-mathematical concept will grow. For example, the "formal" concept of causality may indeed be rare in young children, but a story-concept of causality is clearly common. The latter is hardly unconnected with the former, and ignoring the latter is hardly a sensible way of encouraging development of the former. We see that a concept like causality does not suddenly appear as a formal concept used in history at about sixteen years. Rather, it grows gradually from the uses we see in earliest stories to the more logical forms we see in history and science. Nor can we call the earlier form simpler than the later; it is rather just less specialized. Without use of the earlier forms the later forms will surely be less adequate. This same obvious point might be made about a whole range of concepts that young children are supposed to have no ability to use.

My alternative approach, then, is to focus on the kinds of conceptual abilities children clearly have and use routinely. I will consider just a few features of the kind of stories that children find most engaging, and observe what conceptual abilities must be in place for such stories to be meaningful. From this analysis I will identify those features of stories that can become parts of a model for planning teaching that more fully uses children's conceptual abilities by drawing on the engaging and communicative powers of the story form. If the story is considered as a communicative medium, we will also be able to use our observations about its power and effectiveness to show some of the inadequacies of the objectives —content—methods—evaluation model.

STORY RHYTHM

Stories are narrative units. That they are units is important. They are distinguishable from other kinds of narratives in that they have particular, clear beginnings and ends. The most basic story begins "Once upon a time" and concludes "they lived happily ever after." "Once upon a time" *begins* something and "ever after" does not refer to anything in particular except that what began is now ended. "Once upon a time" creates an expectation of a particular kind. We are told that at some particular time and place something happened. This something will involve a conflict or problem of some kind, which the rest of the story will be taken up resolving.

The story does not deal with anything except the problem set up in the beginning once it is underway. *Everything* in the story is focused on that central task. The weather is not incidental or arbitrary — it will affect either the action or the mood. If it does not, in a good story it will simply be ignored. Stories, then, have clear means of determining what should be included and excluded. We recognize as bad stories those that include things that do not take the story forward. Each such item lets interest sag, and if there are too many of them we stop reading, or watching, or listening.

"What happened next?" has to be answered by an incident or action that takes us towards some complication or resolution of the conflict set up in the beginning. There is, then, at the simplest level a rhythm in stories. They set up an expectation at the beginning, this is elaborated or complicated in the middle, and is satisfied in the end. Stories are tied beginning to end by their satisfying the expectation set up in the beginning. Anything that does not contribute to or fit in with this rhythm is irrelevant to the story and should be excluded. If in *Cinderella* we were to follow one of the ugly sisters through her daily round the story would sag: such events are irrelevant to resolving the particular conflict set up in the beginning of the story.

So we can observe a powerful principle of coherence and a criterion for selecting what is relevant at work in any good story. Such stories hold their power over us as long as all the events stick to and carry forward the basic rhythm. If we consider teaching in light of this cohesive principle of stories we may conclude that the general observation is hardly novel, but it encourages us to look at it in a new way. The principle of organizing a lesson coherently is obvious, but the comparison with the story form suggests new ways in which we might better achieve such coherence. How do we decide what and how much to include in a lesson? More material towards answering this will come in the next section, but here we might draw a first implication from the form of a well-wrought story.

In those stories which children find most engaging there are only those events and details which further the underlying rhythm. Other facts and events that might be connected to those in the story, even if interesting in their own right, are left out. Each irrelevant item, each item that fails to carry forward the story, lets our engagement sag a little. Most stories can obviously bear some of this, but too much and the story is lost. Think of the classic folk-tales. One thing that has happened to them in their centuries of transmission is that they have been honed down to the point where only essential details are included.

Classic folk-tales are, in this regard, a little like jokes. They both set up an expectation in the beginning that is ruthlessly followed to the end. The rhythms of jokes and classic folk-tales are clearly memorable. We might forget stories and jokes, of course, but once started on one the rhythm will usually carry us forward and fit the pieces into place.

A model for teaching that draws on the power of the story, then, will ensure that we set up a conflict or sense of dramatic tension at the beginning of our lessons and units. Thus we create some expectation that we will satisfy at the end. It is this rhythm of expectation and satisfaction that will give us a principle for precisely selecting content. Consider how much content is forgotten after a lesson or unit is finished. What purpose did that forgotten content serve? Well, no doubt, some purpose is served occasionally. We do not want to neglect the fact that some forgotten content nevertheless may remain in the structure of children's understanding of a topic ("I don't remember who opposed the settlement, but I know there was some opposition"). Nevertheless, it is surely reasonable to conclude that much forgotten content — and no doubt much that is remembered too — plays no significant educational role. It remains in Whitehead's sense "inert" (Whitehead, 1929). The implication from this reflection on the power of the story form is that we should concentrate more on simplifying and clarifying our selection of content according to the rhythm set up at the beginning of our lesson or unit. We need, then, to be more conscious of the importance of beginning with a conflict or problem whose resolution at the end can set such a rhythm in motion. Our choice of that opening conflict, then, becomes crucial. Our first consideration must be on what is most important about our topic, and we will identify importance in terms of those profound abstract concepts which children clearly already understand — good/bad, survival/destruction, security /fear, brave/cowardly, and so on.

The rhythms that stories follow are a reflection of further conceptual abilities of children. That is, whatever conceptual abilities are involved in recognizing conflicts and problems and following their elaboration and knowing when they have been satisfactorily resolved, children clearly have. Nor are these trivial intellectual abilities. They are complex and profound. As the study of linguistics has enlarged our understanding of the great complexity of the intellectual task of mastering language, so the study of poetics gives us some hints of the even greater complexity involved in mastery of the story-form. Our educational task is not to analyse these skills in detail, but rather to observe them and recognize more clearly something of the range and profundity of the learning power that children have.

BINARY OPPOSITES

One of the most obvious structural devices we can see in children's stories is the use of binary opposites. Embedded in the story or embodied by the story, are conflicts between good and bad, courage and cowardice, fear and security, and so on. The characters and events embody these underlying abstract conflicts.

These abstract binary opposites serve as criteria for the selection and organization of the content of the story and they serve as the main structuring lines along which the story moves forward. Let us consider these connected functions one at a time.

If we set up a story with a wicked step-mother and a good girl, like *Cinderella*, we begin with a conflict between these embodiments of good and bad. The selection of incidents and further characters, then, will be determined by the need to show the goodness of the one and the badness of the other. The incidents in which the step-mother is cruel to Cinders and favors her own unkind and vain daughters all elaborate the one binary pole. The unfailing kindness and self-sacrificing modesty of Cinderella place her as embodiment of the opposite pole. The story is the embodied conflict of the good and bad. In this way, then, the binary opposites that underlie our story serve as criteria for the selection of the "content" — the characters and incidents — which form the story.

These binary opposites, connectedly, provide the main structural lines along which the story moves forward. Having gathered the conflict at the beginning, we monitor the development of the story through the incidents showing the badness of the step-mother. She tries to frustrate all of Cinderella's wishes and to destroy her one modest hope of attending the Prince's ball. Our expectation is to see contrasting developments of Cinderella's goodness. Once these are vividly clear the conflict can then go forward through the actions of the good helpers, the attempts to frustrate these actions by the bad opposition, and so on to the final satisfying resolution in favor of the good. We even get some mediation in some versions of the story as the step-mother and ugly sisters recognize the error of their ways and, through Cinder's goodness, they too live happily ever after.

Wherever we look in children's stories, and in their own, no doubt derivative, narratives, we find such binary conflicts. We are not here concerned with psychological explanations, so much as simply observing their functions and power in making clear and engaging structures of meaning. Also we should not use such observations to suggest that these features of children's thinking are somehow unique to children. If we pause and consider how we make sense of events we hear about on the news, say, we can see these kinds of binary opposite organizers busily at work. They seem to be the first stage in our organizing and making meaningful new information. If we hear, for example, that there has just been a revolution in an African or South American state, we first search with our binary organizers to orient ourselves to the event. We want to know whether the rebels were supplied with arms by the C.I.A. or whether they had Cuban advisors, for example. That is, we first search for events or facts that allow us to fit the information into our already formed binary ideological structures. If we cannot fit the news account clearly into such structures it remains in danger of being meaningless.

Unfortunately perhaps, the news media that are eager to engage us tend to present information already embedded in such contexts. This tends to restrict our understanding of the world's complexity to the basic unmediated binary opposites of childhood. So our media present political information very much in terms of good and bad competing superpowers, and news-stories that can be fitted to that most easily engaging structure get prominent display, and those that cannot tend to get short shrift. In children's stories, however, the mediation that is appropriate for adults has not yet taken place, and so clarity of meaning requires that we structure information on binary opposites. (This does not mean that we have to present things crudely as good or bad, as I will show in the following chapter.)

So these binary opposites are not only of use in organizing stories, but we see them prominently in all kinds of areas in which we organize and make sense of things. If our concern in planning teaching is to communicate clearly an array of material we might wisely consider how binary opposites might be used to help. For my model then I will build in a way of using binary opposites as a means of organizing and selecting content. Because our aim is educational, unlike that of most news media, we will also want to build in a reminder that we should be seeking mediation of the binary opposites we start with.

AFFECTIVE MEANING

Clearly stories are concerned with affective responses. A good story-teller plays our emotions, as a good violinist plays a violin. We resonate with the rhythm of the binary conflict, the events that carry it forward, and its resolution. Education, seen through the dominant planning and research models, is a largely logical and narrowly rational business. In this view, education is an area where there is little room for our emotional lives. For this reason, the "affective" is usually considered a matter only for the arts — the educational margin or "frills."

As I tried to show in the previous chapter, this view is a product of a misplaced empiricism and of a restricted conception of learning and, not least, of the child. We make sense of the world and experience "affectively" no less than "cognitively." Indeed the separation of the two is a product of the same research programs. Do we make sense of a story affectively or cognitively? Well, of course, both work together. We are not divided into two distinct parts. As we hear melody and harmony as one — though we can separate them in analysis — so we make sense of the world and experience in a unitary way — regardless of what distinctions we might make for research purposes.

The dominant model and its associated research programs have tended to suppress the affective aspects of learning. Consequently they have drawn on only a divided part of children's capacities. A further contribution to teaching that can come from drawing on the story form is a more balanced appeal to children's learning capacities. By using the story form in planning teaching we can reinstate this important and neglected aspect of children's thinking. How stories engage our affective responses, then, is important for us to notice. We will want to build such powers into our model as far as possible, allowing for the differences between typical fictional material and typical classroom instructional material. We can observe at least two ways in which stories engage us affectively.

First, we can observe that stories are largely *about* affective matters — they are about how people feel. These feelings can either provide the motives for actions or they can provide the point and result of actions. If Cinderella's motives were not kind, springing from generous feelings, much of the point of the story would be lost. Also we can readily understand such emotions as causal elements that provide the dynamic of stories. "Jack was angry and decided to get his own back. He stood up, crossed the room, and opened the door." Clearly Jack is going out to get his own back. Such causes of actions present no comprehension problems to young children.

From this observation we can see the importance of human emotions and intentions in making things meaningful. To present knowledge cut off from human emotions and intentions is to reduce its affective meaning. This affective meaning, also, seems especially important in providing *access* to knowledge and engaging us in knowledge. This lesson from our observation of stories will become particularly significant in the discussion of teaching mathematics and sciences in Chapter Four. These are the areas that suffer most from being stripped of their affective associations. We tend to teach mathematics and science as inhuman structures of knowledge, almost taking pride in their logical and inhuman precision. There are two problems with this approach. The first is that it is not true in any sense, the second is that it is educationally disastrous. Later I will discuss ways in which we can rehumanize mathematics and science, seeing the knowledge in its proper, living context of human emotions and intentions.

The second way in which stories engage us affectively follows from the fact that they end. I dwelt earlier on some implications of the obvious point that stories end; they do not just stop but rather they satisfy some conflict set up by their beginning. It is this wrapping up of the story that gives it also a part of its affective power. In life or in history there are no endings; just one damn thing after another. The patterns we impose in order to determine meaning are unlike those of the story. The patterns of our lives or of history are always provisional — something may happen to make us reinterpret, repattern, them. The uniqueness of the story form is that it creates its own world, in which the meaning of events, and thus what we should feel about them, is fixed. Even real-life ugly sisters are on Cinderella's side. We know we have reached the end of the story when we know how to *feel* about all the events and characters that make it up. What is completed by the ending of a good story is the pattern that fixes the meaning and our feelings about the contents.

From this observation we can see that our model needs to provide some way of ending a lesson or unit that has something more in common with the way stories end than with ending because we have "covered" all the content identified as relevant. Our beginning, then, needs to set up some binary conflict or problem and our end needs to resolve it in some way, if we are to take advantage of stories' power to be affectively engaging.

METAPHORS, ANALOGS, AND OBJECTIVES

In the ancient world and through the medieval period people felt their hearts pumping away in their chests just as we do. But they did not know what was going on in there. There are endless accounts in ancient medical speculation and in the myths and stories of the world of what that bumpety-bump in the chest might be. It seems so obvious to us. The heart is a pump. Blood comes out in spurts when we cut an artery because the pump is working at the rate the blood spurts.

The function of the heart became clear only after the invention of the pump. Indeed, as Jonathan Miller (1978, Ch. 5) argues, the function of the heart became *knowable* only after the invention of the pump. Once people understood how a pump worked, they could use that knowledge to make sense of the heart's function. With the advance of technology an analogy was provided which enabled understanding of things which were otherwise mysterious.

We have within us, of course, another functioning organ whose workings are not at all clear to us. We have no adequate mechanical analogs of the brain. We have seen constant attempts to make sense of it in terms of increasingly sophisticated technology. The earliest analogs were natural. Late medieval textbooks represent the brain as a kind of tree with knowledge categorized in various ways as leaves or branches from a trunk representing, often, theology. Later it is represented in terms of clockwork. Then, with a better understanding of the mechanics of the body, we find the brain represented as made up of parts that functioned like muscles — leading to faculty psychology. In this view, the parts, or faculties, of the brain grew and remained limber through exercise, much as a muscle does.

Once the telephone and then telephone exchanges were built we find those providing an analogy for thinking about the brain. This was considered especially appropriate as it was discovered that there was also some kind of electrical activity going on in the brain itself. It seems fair to say that behaviorism, as an overall theory about human behavior, owes more to the telephone exchange than it does to observations of behavior.

To say this about behaviorism is not intended as a contemptuously dismissive criticism. Our thinking is suffused with metaphors and analogies. There is an important sense in which we use the world to think with. We can use the telephone exchange as a tool with which to think about the brain. The analogy is hidden in the theory, but it has provided the means whereby we can get some conceptual grasp on it. We need, however, to be constantly concerned that our analogies are adequate. The pump is an adequate analogy for making sense of the heart. The telephone exchange is, it seems to be becoming increasingly recognized, an inadequate analogy for the brain.

In any scientific field, however, a bad theory is better than no theory at all. It is the inadequate analogy that yields a bad theory, but it is in perceiving the inadequacy of the theory that we can construct a better one. The demise of behaviorism, one might reasonably argue, owes less to the assaults of competing theories, and more to the development of the computer. The computer allows us, analogically, to think about brain functioning in a more sophisticated way than does the telephone exchange. The computer tends thereby to destroy the basis of behaviorism. But it is itself, of course, merely a relatively simple machine, and so provides us still with mechanistic analogies for thinking about the brain.

While it might be fun to continue with such notions, I should return to the point! These comments on metaphorical thinking and the use of analogies are intended as an introduction to reflecting on the adequacy of the dominant model used in planning teaching. In what way? Well, another great technical innovation in this century was the assembly line. Instead of building, for example, an automobile in one place, bringing the components to it and having the same gang of workers do all the different constructive jobs, the assembly line maximized efficiency by the methods now familiar to us all. The various bits and pieces of the automobile were gathered together at different places along the line ready to be slotted into place at the appropriate time. The workers each had specialized functions which they performed in time to the movement of the line. The initial design determined every detail of the process. It is perhaps trite to ask: What does that remind you of?

One thing it might remind us of is the curriculum. We have our overall aim and the problem becomes how best to organize its components into a sequence in order to attain that aim at the end of the process. Education is not so much like an assembly line as that the assembly line provides an analogy which people can use to think about education. Such analogical thinking need not be conscious. No doubt people could understand the heart without conscious reference to the pump, and behaviorists might even resist consciously connecting their conception of behavior with the telephone exchange. But once we understand the pump or the telephone exchange we can make sense of processes which we see in analogous terms. Even though the analogous connection may not be conscious, there is a strong tendency for the language associated with the comprehended process to invade discussion of that which it is used to comprehend. Thus Cubberly early in the century could write that schools are "factories in which the raw products (children) are to be shaped and fashioned into products to meet the various demands of life" (in Callahan, 1962, p. 152).

And so the process of planning teaching can be represented in a model that is an analog of the assembly line. We first design our final product or state our objectives, then we assemble the parts or decide what materials and content we will need in order to achieve those objectives, then we organize workers with appropriate skills along the line or choose the methods appropriate to organize most effectively the teaching of that content, and finally we arrange some means of determining whether each product is satisfactory or we evaluate whether our objectives have been attained.

Now this does not mean that there must be something wrong with planning teaching by means of a model that is an analogous extension of the assembly line. The pump made sense of the heart. The question here, however, is whether the assembly line leads to a model that is adequate for its educational task. The adequacy of such a model is not usually *raised*, however, because we forget that it is an analogous extension from a stage of technological development.

Let us, then, raise the question of whether the dominant model *is* adequate for its educational task. A number of points might be made that can leave us feeling at least uncomfortable about the adequacy of the model. Most generally, derived from the assembly line analogy, is the requirement that the first step in planning teaching requires that one prespecify precisely one's objectives. As the plan of the automobile determines every aspect of the assembly line so our "educational objectives become the criteria by which materials are selected, content is outlined, instructional procedures are developed and tests and examinations are prepared" (Tyler, 1949, p. 3).

Now if we use the dominant model, and its hidden, persuasive analogy, as the means to think about planning teaching, this first requirement will seem obvious. Of course you have to start with precise objectives or you will not know what to do — as you cannot organize an assembly line without a precisely designed automobile to provide the criterion for the construction and organization of the parts and the arrangements of the requisite tools and construction skills. What we have to do here, however, is try to use our understanding of the reality of education to reflect back on the adequacy of this model. This is difficult. Normally we use the model to think *with*; here we are to try to think *about* what we usually think with.

The first simple observation to make is that in education we do not expect, nor should we aim, to have each student become identical "products" in general and in particular we do not expect each student even to learn a particular lesson the same way as any other student. There are endless ways of being and becoming educated. We may try to specify certain necessary conditions, which may form a "core curriculum," but the sheer diversity of individual students and of social and cultural contexts makes even this a most problematic task. Our observation in the classroom shows us the endless and unpredictable ways in which students *use* knowledge. What we properly value in education are these unpredictable and spontaneously creative uses of knowledge. Clearly we can say that the imaginative creativity of children does not prevent us specifying certain objectives precisely. Children can then use in individually unpredictable ways what was the objective of the lesson. But the point here is that it is the unpredictable use, the spontaneity, the creative imagination that is at the educational heart of the matter. What the model does is leave this out in the cold, and suggest that the heart of the matter is the controllable, predictable, prespecifiable part. It is by such means that a model can deform an enterprise it is supposed to serve. This is not an argument against the model, in the sense of a logically convincing refutation. Rather it is one reason why we should feel uncomfortable with the model: what is most valuable is left out, and teachers are not encouraged to focus their attention on it.

Relatedly, if we reflect not just on the diversity of things a teacher might hope to have happen in an average class, but the ways in which all kinds of associations of ideas, particular hobbies or interests, wonder and humour, that might purely incidentally be stimulated, we may consider whether the reality of educational engagements is inappropriately represented as planned means working carefully along a prespecified path to precisely delineated objectives. Of course we can organize our curricula and lessons this way. But such a process seems not to *fit* some obvious features of education.

In the assembly line, and the analogous model, the product is made up of the pieces put together in the right way in the right sequence. The educated person is not merely the accumulated product of all that has been learned. The more basic problem at the heart of this objection is subtle and, again, not a compelling argument so much as a point of view from which the inadequacy of the model is pointed to. The assembly line model sees the educational product as a carefully planned accumulation of parts. Human understanding, however, does not seem to accumulate this way.

Perhaps I can better point to the inadequacy of the old-technology derived model by contrasting it by analogy with a newer technology. In the old model human understanding is represented as analogous to a two-dimensional picture. In order to compose the picture we need only get all the pieces together and fit them in their places. But if we think of human understanding as more like a hologram than a two dimensional picture, we see the poverty of the older view. If a hologram is broken in pieces, each piece contains an image of the whole. The laser will not show simply a part of the picture, but will show a fuzzy image of the whole. As pieces are added the whole picture becomes clearer. The curriculum is not adequately conceptualized if it is viewed as like a two dimensional picture that can be completed by putting the pieces together one by one. Rather it is a matter of coalescence and increasing clarity, in whose composition linear processes are inadequate.

My point, again, is not that the dominant model is in any sense *wrong*. Rather, it embodies a way of thinking about education, and encourages ways of thinking about teaching, that are in profound and subtle ways *inadequate*. The alternative I will describe in the following chapter is also, of course, inadequate, but its virtue I think is that it is less inadequate than what I am proposing it should replace. (Without the dominant model, of course, there could not have been this recommended alternative.)

The assembly line has become a fairly general metaphor for dehumanizing working conditions. Some automakers have tried a number of alternatives to the assembly line in order to reduce the deadening and deskilled routines it encourages. The assembly line is saved, however, by its perfectly attuned robot servants. The dehumanizing carries over, it seems to me, into the planning model for teaching derived by analogy from the assembly line. It has tended to reduce and deform education into a process of accumulating sequences of measurable knowledge and skills. It has tended to suppress, in the name of greater efficiency, the organic complexity of education, and to disguise the fact that we can adequately measure or evaluate only relatively trivial aspects of education.

In conclusion to this rather imprecise discussion — imprecise, because we are dealing with things we have no adequate analogies to enable us to make precise sense of — we might briefly reflect on how well the assembly line works as an analogy for telling a story. Part of my point is the sense of strain we feel thinking of a story in terms of an assembly line. And yet we can do so: we need to have our product or objective clear at the beginning, we need to organize the content, decide on our narrative procedures, and prepare some way of discovering whether we have successfully got the story across. The point is that this just is not a very useful way to think about how to plan telling a story. The analogy at the basis of the comparison simply does not fit very well. It misses the point of the story form in the way that a clockwork orange misses the point of fruit. What I will turn to now is trying to show that telling a story is a better analogy than the assembly line for teaching and that the story form provides a more adequate model for planning teaching.

CONCLUSION

Telling a story is a way of establishing meaning. Fictional stories tend to be concerned very largely with affective meaning, whereas in education our concern is more comprehensive. We want "cognitive" and "affective" meaning together. Because the dominant model has tended to emphasize the cognitive at the expense of the affective, drawing on some aspects of the story form for planning teaching can enable us to achieve a better balance. The result in practice of such abstract matters is clearer access to material for children and greater engagement with it.

The sense of story I am dealing with here is not so much the typical fictional kind, but something nearer to what a newspaper editor means when he asks his reporter "What's the story on this?" The editor is asking for an account of the particular events embedded in some more abstract context which readers already understand. The editor basically wants to know how the particulars fit into some binary conflict: How do these particulars give body to the ongoing story of good vs. bad, or security vs. danger, or political right vs. left, etc. The editor's question is one about how this particular knowledge is to be made meaningful and engaging to readers. So when I advocate use of some features of the story form it is in order to make new knowledge meaningful and engaging to children.

I will want to build into my model then some means of establishing at least some degree of story-like rhythm. This requires a particular kind of beginning that sets up an expectation, and a conclusion that satisfies this expectation. Such an overall form wraps the beginning and the end of a lesson or unit more tightly together than is usual. The new model also will be alert to the importance of underlying binary opposites for engaging interest and carrying it along. They also will provide a key criterion for the selection and organization of content.

I have spent some time discussing the inappropriateness of thinking about teaching by means of a model analogous to the assembly line because the major "heresy" of my model is that it does not begin with a statement of objectives. Indeed, objectives are not mentioned anywhere. In telling a story one does not begin by stating objectives, and yet stories are wonderful tools for efficiently organizing and communicating meaning. A major point of this book is that teaching is centrally concerned with efficiently organizing and communicating meaning, and so we will sensibly use a planning model derived from one of the world's most powerful and pervasive ways of doing this. Objectives based models are products of a particular phase of industrialization. They are the result of attempts to technologize teaching in inappropriate ways. They result in clockwork oranges. It is time to move to something more fruitful.

CHAPTER 3

An Alternative Model

INTRODUCTION

Well, enough of the inadequacies of the presently domi-nant principles and model. Among the alternative principles that have come from our discussion so far are the need to begin by identifying what most matters about a topic — in the "What's the story on this?" sense; the need to structure the topic on the powerful binary abstract concepts that children so easily grasp and grasp new knowledge with; the need to lay out our unit or lesson in a story form; the need to conclude by satisfying the expectation or resolving, perhaps by mediating, the conflict set up at the beginning.

It is not difficult now to put these alternative principles to work in a new model for planning teaching. Following Tyler's example, I will lay out the model as a series of ques-tions. Providing answers to these questions produces a lesson or unit plan. After laying out the model I will discuss how to use it, and make some comments about it. Rather than do this in the abstract, I will take two examples.

First I will show how the model might be used to pro-duce a plan for teaching a unit on Communities for six-year-olds. Then I will use it to plan a lesson on the Vikings for children of the same age. By planning a topic which is com-mon in curricula in North America and Australia during the early grades, and increasingly common in Great Britain and Ireland, I hope to show how the alternative principles embodied in this alternative model produce a significantly different learning experience for children. I hope readers will agree that it is likely to be more educationally valuable than what typically results from using some form of the presently dominant model.

My purpose in providing a brief plan for a lesson on the Vikings is to exemplify some of the principles discussed in the previous two chapters. The influence of research focused almost exclusively on a limited range of logical skills has led to the exclusion of topics from ancient or medieval history from the early years of schooling. There are, of course, other arguments given for beginning with less "distant" topics — and I will consider some of them in Chapter Five — but significant among the reasons for the exclusion of such a topic is the claim that young children cannot understand it in any meaningful way. It is supposed to require concepts which young children do not typically "develop" until much later. Also, by applying the *ad hoc* principle that learning proceeds from the known to the unknown, it is only after a number of years of schooling that children's understanding can be "expanded" to grasp a topic which involves so much that is different from their daily experience.

The two examples are "social studies" topics, because these are most easily accessible to all readers. I have suggested that this model can be applied also to subjects which are not so rich in events, such as mathematics and science. In the following Chapter, then, I will consider how this model can be used in planning teaching in various curriculum areas.

APPLYING THE MODEL

The principles discussed in the first two chapters have implications not only for how we should plan teaching but clearly, as part of our planning perhaps, they direct us towards some kinds of content rather than others. The very first question of the model implies that if we cannot find anything affectively engaging in a topic then we should go no further. That is, the question provides also a criterion for inclusion in or exclusion from our curriculum. Now we can find something affectively engaging about almost anything, but clearly some things lend themselves better than others if this

The Story Form Model

1. Identifying importance:

   What is most important about this topic?
   Why should it matter to children?
   What is affectively engaging about it?

2. Finding binary opposites:

   What powerful binary opposites best catch the
   importance of the topic?

3. Organizing content into story form:

   3.1 What content most dramatically embodies
   the binary opposites, in order to provide
   access to the topic?

   3.2 What content best articulates the topic into a
   developing story form?

4. Conclusion:

   What is the best way of resolving the dramatic
   conflict inherent in the binary opposites?
   What degree of mediation of those opposites is
   it appropriate to seek?

5. Evaluation:

   How can one know whether the topic has been
   understood, its importance grasped,
   and the content learned?

is a criterion for selecting content. This is a matter I will discuss in Chapter Five, but I raise it here because the first example — Communities — is a topic I would prefer to leave out of my early school curriculum. I will explain why in Chapter Five, but essentially it is because I think such a topic is not easy to make *both* meaningful *and* educationally valuable for young children. I nevertheless have chosen it simply because it is a very common topic in many parts of the western world during the early school years. That is, teachers are familiar with such a topic, they have to teach it because it is prescribed, and they have plans for teaching it which can be readily compared with the product of applying this model. I want to show also that one can plan a unit on medieval history which is accessible, engaging, and educationally valuable for young children. The reason for juxtaposing the two will be brought out in Chapter Five. But the point here is to exemplify the model with varied material, so let us turn to that.

I am recommending that we should approach a unit on Communities as a story to be told, rather than as a set of objectives that is to be attained. We should remember that stories can be true as well as fictional, and that shaping material into a story form may involve simplification but need not at all involve falsification. Also we should remember that in a well-wrought story there is room for detailed knowledge, and inference, and discovery processes, and much else. We might orient ourselves by imagining a newspaper editor on some distant planet asking his investigative reporters from Earth "What's the story on these communities? What am I gonna tell our readers?"

1.   **Identifying importance:**
        What is most important about this topic?
        Why should it matter to children?
        What is affectively engaging about it?

Communities are networks of supports, protections, affections, beliefs, and so on. They are held together by our mutual needs and desires, and they are threatened by our tendency to value our needs and desires excessively highly and those of others excessively lowly. They are also threatened by natural catastrophes that smash the complex network of supports, protections, affections, beliefs, and so on. Communities are the products of unwritten social contracts we enter into with each other. These generate a kind of social organism that protects us from destruction and enables the satisfaction of our desires.

To say that children are parts of a community and the community is vitally important, does not establish that the topic can easily be made affectively engaging. Children take their everyday lives too much for granted to be able to reflect on them in a way that makes them intellectually engaging. Fish probably do not find water very interesting, until they are pulled out of it. Perhaps this observation provides us with one way towards making the topic affectively engaging. Children tend to take their community routines as "natural," so we must find a way of showing those routines as vividly dramatic, and not simply as prosaic everyday experience. Underlying the prosaic routines that form the visible surface of our communities there are vital needs being met, desperate fears being allayed, incredible hopes being made possible, and so on. To make our topic affectively engaging, it is this dramatic — and real — level underlying the routines of community life that must be exposed. This is what is important; this is the real story on human communities.

Now we need not present this underlying reality in some nightmare-inducing form as "horrors from the deep." But at the same time we need to recall our earlier discussion of how children use the most dramatic and powerful concepts to make sense of things. The typical presentation of this topic dwells on the prosaic routines and so remains affectively unengaging and, in any profound sense, largely meaningless. In order to justify the place of this topic in the early school curriculum we need to show that it can be structured on the kinds of powerful concepts children use to grasp new knowledge. Let us see whether we can catch something of what is really important about communities in terms of these concepts.

2. Finding binary opposites:
    What powerful binary opposites best catch
    the importance of the topic?

What binary opposites best catch and allow us to expose
the underlying drama of everyday community living? We
need to see the prosaic parts — milk delivery, the mail, shopping, roads and telephones, etc. — as one of the greatest
achievements of human ingenuity and planning. What is at
stake in a community is not just our superficial comforts and
conveniences but life itself. If our communities cease to function, we die.

There are a number of binary opposites we might choose
to express aspects of this view of the function of communities. Why not pause from reading for a minute and see
how many you can come up with, and which you would
choose as most generally useful.

Given what I have identified as important about the
topic, I will use the binary opposites of survival/destruction.
We could have focused on a slightly less dramatic level with
security/danger. We might have considered the dynamics of
a community through competition/cooperation. Other,
perhaps more superficial aspects of the community might be
exposed by use of dependence/independence. An historical
perspective might have been brought to the fore through the
choice of change/stability.

We have reached survival/destruction by looking at the
topic of communities through the prominent conceptual
forms the child already has in place. Our model directs us to
these by demanding first that we focus on what is most important about a topic. One of the *ad hoc* principles I did not
pursue in the first chapter is the claim that children's
understanding proceeds from the simple to the complex. This
has encouraged teachers and curriculum designers to begin
with the simpler, more superficial aspects of topics. From
observations of children's stories, it seems clear that "from
the simple to the complex" is, again, inadequate as an account of the development of children's understanding. Our
earliest understanding is of profound things. One might say
that we learn some of the most important, profound, and

powerful concepts very early, and thereafter we refine and elaborate them. So, perhaps ironically in the face of the presently dominant *ad hoc* principles, it is the most profound and important aspects of a topic that need to be brought to the fore if we want young children to understand it.

3. Organizing content into story form:
    3.1 **What content most dramatically embodies the binary opposites, in order to provide access to the topic?**

We need to begin our story-unit with an event, or incident, or example that most vividly shows communities as not just people doing different jobs and depending on each other for various commodities, but rather as a matter of survival against destruction. We might begin by setting out a scenario for the children. Suppose when we wake up tomorrow our village/town/city is cut off from the rest of North America/Australia/Europe? Say there is a huge steel wall all around our community. All the roads just run to a stop against it. It cuts off the telephone wires. It is too high to fly over, and too deep to dig under, and too thick and strong to smash. It cuts off all the pipes under the ground too. After giving the children a chance to discuss the characteristics of the wall, the teacher can focus back to the point that it cuts us off from everyone outside our own immediate community. If the water pipes that lead to our taps are cut, where will we get water? How long would our food last? What would happen if there was no electricity and the gasoline runs out?

Either as a follow-on discussion, or as an alternative, we might extend the scenario by saying that the next day, or a few days later, we wake up to find another steel wall around our house/apartment/igloo? Now what happens?

Well, no doubt experienced teachers might come up with a dozen better openers. The point is that we need a beginning activity that gives dramatic point to the concept of a community as a machine which people have made to help our survival and fend off destruction. It is something vitally important for our daily survival. We cannot simply take it for granted.

3.2　What content best articulates the topic into a developing story form?

This question directs us not simply to gather in a list all the things we consider relevant to the topic of Communities. Rather it requires that we select content according to the binary opposites chosen to express the most important aspects of the topic. Each item will be selected in order to give further expression and elaboration to our survival/destruction organizers. As in any good story we must keep to our plot line or else we will dissipate meaning. Our plot line is given in the conflict set up between the forces that enable our survival in the face of the various threats of destruction. This model requires that all content be tied to this line.

No doubt much of the content of this unit will be similar to that used when it is planned by any other model. The differences will be in organization, in the focus on particular aspects of the content rather than others, and also in tone. The tone determined by this model requires that the unit be taken *seriously*. This does not mean that it need be dull and sombre, rather it means that the content must be recognized as important. A lot turns on whether children become educated or not; it is a serious business, and this model reinforces this fact at every stage of planning.

If we consider food, for example, it will be insufficient to describe the kinds of foods available in a local supermarket and the routes they take to get there. Our binary opposites focus attention on food as a means of survival, and also on the threats of destruction. Now obviously when dealing with food this is always implied. Here, however, it has to be made explicit and central. Our unit is not about food, but about survival. That is, the focus is on what variety of foods we need to survive. We can then distinguish between necessities, and the abundance available at a western supermarket whose purpose is to satisfy unessential matters of taste. Having made such a distinction our binary organizers direct us to focus on the essentials. We will then focus on the problems in getting those to the supermarket, and the threats to that process. We already know what will happen if these necessities fail to be delivered regularly, but we can discount the steel wall as a realistic threat. The steel wall, however, is a kind of analogy for all the other threats. Our focus will be on the threats to crops and how these are defended against (weather, petroleum products, fertilizers, insecticides, etc.), on the problems of keeping food from rotting during transportation (perhaps including here the dramatic story of the first refrigerated railcars), on the threats to the transportation system (vast systems of rail and road machinery, and industries producing railcars and trucks, and the threats to the supply lines for all the components, and fuel supply problems).

One product of this manner of presenting the way our community makes food available to its members, is that it shows the supermarket not as a routine prosaic aspect of community life, but as one of the wonders of the world. The *ad hoc* principles disputed earlier suggest that we should expand outwards from what is familiar to children. A more important early educational principle has been stated by Bertrand Russell as the need to destroy the tyranny of the local over the imagination. The educational achievement is not to make the strange seem familiar, but to make the familiar seem strange. It is seeing the wonderful that lies hidden in what we take for granted that matters educationally. Provincialism is education's first and most tenacious enemy. This model builds in principles to help us combat taking the world for granted. In this case the supermarket is seen as a miracle of human ingenuity and organizational skill. To properly grasp that miracle it has to be seen in the context of the threats to its achievement and continuation.

Again, this need not be presented as a nightmare-inducing scenario. What is educationally important is letting the children's binary conceptual structures — developed, defined, and elaborated in significant part by their use in fantasy stories — grasp the real world. Fantasy, in this view, is a kind of early conceptual workshop, where powerful conceptual tools are forged and elaborated; the educational task is then to use these powerful tools in making sense of reality. We do not attach them to reality if we present only the routine surfaces of everyday life. There is nothing there for children to get much of a grip on. It is by introducing knowledge organized in terms of these powerful underlying concepts that we provide children with a grasp on reality.

We continue to use survival/destruction as the criterion for selecting content for our unit. We will look at the range of possible content, not as a list of "relevant" topics, but as a coordinated set of strategies for survival. Thus we can consider our basic human needs and consider the ways that the community fulfills them and defends against potential threats to them.

So we might, for example, consider the role of servicemen. It is not just that a cheerful man comes and fixes mummy's drier when it breaks down, but that this man or woman and many others are the repositories of skilled knowledge needed for our survival in a technological society. One obviously does not present it to children in these terms, but our binary organizers direct us to see the serviceman in terms of our plot line. We are directed also to consider the threats to those service functions. What if the machines stop and there is no-one who knows how to fix them? How do communities ensure there are people who know how to fix all the different kinds of machines we rely on? It is appropriate in this context to consider not just an idealized view of there being so many helpers in the community, but rather that most people are absolutely dependent on the machines running, and being fixed. Again, the system of defences against our technological traps are seen not as routines but wonders of complex organization. There is nothing quite as amazing as our communities — may well be a part of the lesson of this unit.

Well, I am in danger of going on endlessly elaborating the same point with lots of similar examples. I hope it is clear how our survival/destruction binary opposites can be used to select and organize the content that will carry our story forward. Each part adds to the image of the community as a complex machine designed to defend us against destruction.

I chose that binary pair as basic organizers as a result of deciding what seemed to me most important to teach children about communities. It will be clear that another side of the power of such organizers in selecting and organizing content is that they also serve to exclude a great deal. They provide a perspective that will give greater prominence to the role of police than to the role of, say, mail delivery. That is, all those community functions designed most directly to support survival against threats will be more centrally located on our plot line. This need not exclude the mailman and community centre, of course. By identifying ties of affection as a basic human need, the role of the mailman becomes included in our plot. Again, however, our educational purpose will be served by making the familiar strange; by making the routines of mail delivery comprehensible as a truly amazing achievement. From almost anywhere in the world, for a very small amount of money, one can have a letter delivered to almost anywhere else. Perhaps the amazement of this achievement can be brought out by considering the great steps towards the present routine — the British Penny Black postage stamp, the pony express, the arrangements for mail delivery with other countries and the Universal Postal Union (postage stamps from around the world acclaiming this achievement might be displayed).

Elsewhere I have written about differences between socializing and educating (Egan, 1983b). In teaching a unit on Communities the differences become important. In socializing we aim to make students familiar with their environment, at home in its routines, comfortable with its norms and values and the social expectations to which they should conform. This is, I think, the usual aim of teaching about Communities in early years. My alternative model, by demanding first that we reflect on the importance of the topic for the child's education, will tend to bring educational considerations to the fore. Socializing most effectively happens simply by living in societies day by day, and schools are generally rather ineffective socializing institutions when they try to teach what is best learned from out-of-school experience. And further, by attempting to perform the socializing role at which they are ineffective, schools tend to undercut their educational role (Nyberg and Egan, 1981). This is what we often see in the teaching of subjects like Communities. If a person does not know what a supermarket is and how it functions generally in society by age fifteen or twenty, it will not be due to whether or not the topic was well taught at age six.

The educational task is to ensure that when fifteen-year-olds look at a supermarket, they will see it not as a routine part of the everyday environment, but as a small miracle. Their understanding must be such as to see, not just the superficial surface, but to have that surface as a symbol for a rich appreciation of the wonderful achievements that underlie it.

I have discussed the content very much at an adult level, relying on teachers being better able than I am to work out ways of implementing the principles for the classroom. I should, nevertheless, perhaps reiterate that the point is not to teach children about survival and destruction. Underlying this whole alternative approach is the observation that children already know those concepts in some profound way. The point is to *use* them to make sense of new material. Clearly children may not be able to provide explicit definitions of "survival" or "destruction," but we can be sure they know them because they easily make sense of stories whose meaning requires understanding of such concepts.

While the choice of binary opposites provides us with powerful organizers, it does not determine the way we value a topic. In the way I have discussed organizing the content so far, it is clear that we are seeing the Community as positively valuable without any qualifications. We could organize the content quite differently to give quite a different view. For the sake of example I will move to the other extreme, and draw on another important way of making things engaging for young children.

I have already discussed the importance of children being able to make sense of things by means of their most highly developed ways of "grasping" the world. Among these "grasping" or grappling tools are the ability to make sense of things in terms of human intentions, emotions, hopes, fears, etc. By *personalizing* the impersonal we can use these tools.

We might, then, vivify our image of the Community as an organism, by suggesting that children think of the community as a creature. Going back in time the teacher can describe it (using visual representations) as a small creature who settled down by the local river. As the years went by it grew by drinking the pure water and dirtying it as it passed through, and by eating away at the surrounding land. It became bigger and fatter and more monstrous, and grew faster and faster. It sent tentacles (roads) deep into the countryside to get food from more and more distant places to satisfy its ever-growing appetite, destroying the natural woods and meadows. Some tentacles ripped up the land to get minerals and fuels which it ate in its factories, dirtying further the land, air, and water. It became bigger and noisier. It is greedy and selfish, sprawling across hills and valleys, eating everything in its way. It, like us, is trying to grow and survive and overwhelm the threats to its destruction.

I am not here recommending one or the other way of presenting the material. Rather, I am trying to show only that using this model does not commit us to any particular value position. Its contribution is that it helps to select and organize material to be more meaningful and engaging to children and more beneficial. As in a good story, this model guides us to tie each element to the strong and clear underlying structure, which is made from affectively engaging binary opposites.

4. Conclusion:
   What is the best way of resolving the dramatic conflict inherent in the binary opposites?
   What degree of mediation of those opposites is it appropriate to seek?

Following this model we need to find some way of bringing our unit to a close that is more like the way a story ends than simply stopping because we have run out of material. The survival/destruction theme has provided a structure to our unit, and so in conclusion we need to resolve in some way the dramatic conflict set up between them. The resolution may take the form of a mediation or as a confirmation of a particular perspective.

A confirmation of the wonderful achievement of the Community in providing for our needs and desires might be presented by means of a concluding story which brings together all the material dealt with. Such a story might have as its wicked protagonist a monster who tries to destroy a community. The body of the story could be made up of the monster's various attacks and the community's defences. The monster sets fires, the fire brigade puts them out; smashes up roads to prevent food coming in, the repair crews fix them; and so on.

Alternatively the children, in small groups perhaps, might argue about which feature of the community contributes most towards its protection. The teacher might prepare "roles"; giving each group a card with the feature it is to argue for and some main points around which it might build a case. For example: Police protect us from robbers and murderers, and keep the traffic moving safely (so that goods can be driven to the stores and we can drive to the stores to get food); Schools provide us with knowledge so that people can read and write and so survive in our literate society, and provide an introduction to the arts of civilized living that make communities work, and provide introductions to technical skills necessary for keeping our machines running. Cards can be prepared on all the other agencies of the community touched on in the unit. The teacher's role in such a guided discussion can be to point out that these "roles" are not really in competition, but that they cooperate to keep the community going.

We might decide to conclude by seeking a mediation between our binary organizers. To do this we would need to show that a community is dynamic and alive as a result of its constant struggle to survive. Only by being energetic in fending off all the threats to survival does the community exist as such. The community lives then in the balance of survival/destruction. If the threats all vanished, we would no longer need communities. We can see how features of communities change and ,sometimes evaporate as particular threats to survival disappear. We no longer need walls around our communities, and so we do not need night watchmen and all those others whose community function was either building, care, or guarding of the walls. We no longer need horses for transportation, and so the feeding, protection, shoeing, etc., of horses no longer provides employment to community members.

No doubt experienced teachers can come up with a number of other ways of implementing these ideas. The guiding principle here is that we need to resolve in some degree the conflict between survival and destruction. We need to work out some way of bringing together the material dealt with in the body of the unit and showing clearly the relationship between the binary organizers. As we began with some vivid exposition of the dramatic conflict between the two, so we end with some vivid resolution of that conflict. Above I have suggested conclusions that show all the aspects of the community working in dynamic cooperation to keep the complex social organization in equilibrium.

5. **Evaluation:**
   How can one know whether the topic has been understood, its importance grasped, and the content learned?

The important educational task of this unit is to attach children's concepts of survival/destruction to knowledge about their community. By this means they will be able to make sense of their community as something dynamic, wonderful, and important. They attach profound abstract concepts, perhaps mainly elaborated in fantasy and stories, to reality. How do we evaluate our success at this?

The danger, so evident in so much test-driven teaching practice, is that we accept as evidence of learning success something other than what is educationally important. Because it is so difficult to work out how to measure the educationally important achievement, we measure instead what seems an index of that achievement. The easiest thing to measure is what knowledge is remembered some short time after the unit is completed. This kind of measure accounts for a great deal of educational evaluation, and is taken as an index of the more important lesson taught.

We can, of course, learn much from sensitive evaluation, but this model does not contribute anything significant that I can see to the evaluation of the learning the model encourages. Because of its focus on more complex and important learning, this model might be seen as making the evaluator's task that little bit harder. But in general the usual array of evaluation procedures can be brought to bear at the conclusion of, or during, a lesson or unit.

A LESSON ON THE VIKINGS

For this second example of the model at work I have chosen a topic normally considered inappropriate for elementary school children. Among the reasons for excluding it from the elementary school curriculum are those which I have discussed above as derived from the presently influential *ad hoc* principles. Part of my purpose here, then, is to demonstrate that one can indeed organize a lesson on the Vikings in a way that is meaningful, engaging, and educationally valuable for young children.

This lesson, let us assume, is a part of a unit on World History. Let us further assume that we are presenting this unit as the story of a struggle for civilization against barbarism. Such an overall binary theme would then focus us particularly onto topics in which that struggle is most evident; hence the Vikings. (We could alternatively or additionally, look at World History as a story of the struggle between freedom and tyranny, or security and danger, or knowledge and ignorance, or any number of themes, each of which would focus attention onto somewhat different historical material.)

It may be thought that young children will likely not have much grasp on such concepts as "civilization" or "barbarism." This may appear to be a double problem for the model, as it is not just a matter of getting children to learn them, as that these are the concepts we are expecting them to learn *with*. That is, the basic assumption of this model is that children have these concepts available to use in grasping new knowledge about the world.

Again, while children typically would be unable to define explicitly what "civilization" or what "barbarism" is, there is a clear sense in which they profoundly understand such concepts. "Civilization" is, most simply, the forms of behavior which make living together most generally easy; tolerance, self-control and self-restraint, ability to share, willingness to contribute to the general welfare. "Barbarism" is the lack of these civilizing virtues. In families, in the classroom, in the school yard, and in the neighborhood, children learn about such things — well or badly. While they may not know what "tolerance" or its opposite are explicitly, they understand them precisely in their exclusion from games on arbitrary grounds. They understand "self-retraint" and its opposite in their own or other children's berserk behavior. When, for example, they learn about the Viking "berserkers," they will have no trouble understanding that warriors can fight with a frenzied fury in which they do not calculate as in normal behavior the consequences of their actions. Family life and the school yard provide a microcosm of the forces that have shaped the history of the world and its struggle for civilized life against the ever-present forces of barbarism. The educational task for this lesson is to extend their concepts from their local experience and attach them to one part of the real history of their world.

1. Identifying importance:
    What is most important about the topic?
    Why should it matter to children?
    What is affectively engaging about it?

I have answered these questions largely in the introduction above. What matters about this topic at this time in children's lives is that they begin to understand that the conflicts they see in their families and neighborhoods and schools, and the conflicts they feel within themselves, are analogous to those that have shaped history. In addition they will begin to understand that civilized life is a tenuous thing that has survived, where it has survived, by the skin of its teeth. Our lesson may be designed in order to make this point vividly, and spell out that the same barbaric forces are present all the time and that the values of tolerance, self-retraint, and so on, are essential for all of us to practice as prerequisites to civilized life. What is affectively engaging about all this is that the emotions, impulses, hopes, and fears which animate this episode of history are vividly a part of children's lives.

2. Finding binary opposites:
    What powerful binary opposites best catch
    the importance of the topic?

This lesson is one of a series, each of which carries forward the theme of civilization struggling against barbarism. This is one perspective through which the human story can be told. Though all aspects of the struggle between Vikings and the realms to their south, west, and east cannot be told from this perspective, it allows us to tell something important about those times. As this lesson is a part of a larger unit, we will build it upon the binary opposites of the overarching story. Each lesson, then, serves to carry forward and add to the general unit, much as an episode in a "soap-opera" carries forward a general story while being a mini-story itself. So we will organize our lesson on the Vikings in terms of the struggle between civilization and barbarism.

   3.   **Organizing content into story form:**
        **3.1   What content most dramatically embodies
             the binary opposites, in order to provide
             access to the topic?**

We might begin with an image of the monks at Lindisfarne at work. Part ' of their role was to preserve the knowledge left by the now destroyed Roman Empire. (A look at which might have been the subject of a previous lesson.) Examples of monks' writing could be shown — perhaps the enlarged pages of the Book of Kells might serve. The monks can be shown working in their fields, tending their animals, studying and writing in a scriptorium. Then strangers are seen. The strangers are carrying weapons and are running. The monks outside run back to their monastery. They bar the doors. Nothing can keep the Vikings out. They break in, kill the monks, steal whatever looks valuable, burn and destroy everything else, and take the novices (young monks) as slaves.

This first attack was in 793 A.D., long after English kingdoms had been set up. It is enough for children to place the incident in a causal sequence a long time after the Roman Empire fell, and a long, long time ago. Our beginning can conclude with the questions people at the time had after the first raids. Who were the Vikings? Where did they come from?

This opening incident needs to dramatize the contributions the monks were making to civilization and the wanton destructiveness of the Vikings. That the idea of a monk and preserver of knowledge from a past better time is easily made comprehensible to children can been seen from the analogous image of Obi-wan Kenobi in *Star Wars*. This dweller in the wilderness with relics of a past civilization is not, of course, the same as a monk, and Darth Vadar's Storm Troopers are not the same as Vikings, but the concepts in each case are no less comprehensible. And of course children may not be able to fully understand what a monk is, but within the story the meaning of monk and monastery begins to take on definition.

3.2   What content best articulates the topic into a developing story form?

The next part of the lesson can be spent briefly explaining that Europe was made up of realms with lots of kings each ruling over lands made up mainly of small towns and villages. If a king did not know where or when an attack was coming he could do little to protect his towns and villages. The Vikings raided without warning. They were *berserk* fighters; fearless themselves and merciless to others. Women and children were slaughtered as the Vikings burned and destroyed everything they could not steal.

We need to focus our story, and might choose to make central to this lesson the remarkable figure of Alfred the Great. Because of our theme we will need to bring out the fact that Alfred was a beacon of civilization in a barbaric time. From boyhood his life was spent fighting and running from Vikings, fighting and being defeated by them, and fighting them again and again. Despite this he gathered around him scholars. He himself learned to read — a rare accomplishment in those days — and later in life learned Latin. He gathered documents and organized translations into English. He set up a school for the children of his lords. This strange warrior king, almost always on the move, struggling to hold his kingdom together, was a founder of English cultural life. We can convey some image of this to children by stressing his love of knowledge and the arts of gentle and civilized life; and that, even so, he was, reluctantly, one of the greatest warriors.

Our central story, then, will be of Alfred's constant defeats and the cruelty and destructiveness of the various Viking raiding parties. Children should learn the names of Viking leaders like Ragnar Lothbrok, Eric Bloodaxe, Ivar the Boneless, Halfdan, and Guthrum. In their conquests they destroyed monasteries across England, destroying the civilizing knowledge contained in their manuscripts. In a story one does not need to *explain* why a manuscript is valuable if the story *shows* its value by the horror people felt at its loss. The efforts of Alfred to preserve and add to the manuscripts of the English again *shows* their importance in a way that does not need further explanation.

A key incident in our story will be Alfred's hiding in the marsh-island of Athelney. From there he sent out the call to his nobles and churls. They came from far and wide, until Alfred could lead out an army that destroyed the power of Guthrum at Edington.

Instead of trying to kill every last enemy, Alfred aimed to civilize them too, and to live in peace with them. He required that Guthrum become a Christian and agreed to his settling with the remains of his army in the east of England. In 899 King Alfred died in peace, recognized as King of the English as no king before him had been.

Clearly one would not tell the story of Alfred in these terms. Again, I am assuming that teachers will see many ways that this basic plot line can be taught. My concern here is to show how our basic binary theme helps us to select and organize the content which will best convey what is important. In order to teach such a lesson to children certain visual resources are desirable. Because we have for so long excluded such topics from our early school curricula, and assumed that children can understand only the local, the immediate, the concrete, the simple, and what they can actively manipulate, we lack appropriate resources that are easily accessible. If the principles I am supporting in this book become more widely accepted, then perhaps we may see such materials produced in profusion.

Here I want only to lay out the way in which one might organize a lesson on the Vikings in a story form and using concepts that children would find easily comprehensible, and indeed engaging.

4. **Conclusion:**
   What is the best way of resolving the dramatic conflict inherent in the binary opposites?
   What degree of mediation of those opposites is it appropriate to seek?

One might conclude in a number of ways. We could deal with Alfred's achievement in preserving and extending civilization even among the Vikings. In such a conclusion we might consider that Alfred was more ready to be defeated and get up and fight again than the Vikings were ready to defeat him. Civilized life, in his view, offers more to live for and more to fight for than does barbarism. Even the victorious barbarians come to see it in the end. It is easier to destroy than to build. But something in the joy of building outlasts the shallow pleasure of destruction.

Perhaps better might be a mediation, in which we recognize the Viking contributions as well. We might note that our knowledge of the Viking raids comes mainly from the monks' writings. They present them as simply evil — a curse sent for people's sins. We might in contrast consider how just a few thousand men — twice or four times, or however many times, more than there are children in the school, set out in open ships from their villages in Scandinavia. A ship could carry perhaps forty men and sometimes their horses too. In a few years they destroyed much of London and Paris, Hamburg and Antwerp, Bordeaux and Seville, Morocco and the Rhone villages. They founded Russia, and besieged Constantinople. They settled and took over Normandy, Sicily and Iceland. They discovered Greenland and America, and united England and Denmark under Cnut. Through their raids Moorish slaves were to be found in their town of Dublin, and piles of English coins were found in Russia. They were afraid of nothing; neither kings, armies, God, or the cold. In the end, they won the battle for

England, when the Viking descendant William of Normandy conquered the country in 1066. Their fierce energy contributed to rebuilding the civilization they very nearly destroyed. It is an odd story, in which perhaps civilization conquered the Vikings in the end.

5. **Evaluation:**
   How can one know whether the topic has been understood, its importance grasped, and the content learned?

I have nothing much to add to the comments made under this section in the unit on Communities. We need to be careful that we focus our evaluation on what is important. Do the children understand further the constant battle between civilization and barbarism? Has the story of Alfred and the Vikings refined further their understanding of civilization and of barbarism? Degrees of refinement of understanding are difficult to measure.

CONCLUSION
Here, then, are outline plans for a unit and a lesson using the alternative model. What it does is focus our attention on what matters most about any topic and direct us to articulate what matters on the kind of powerful concepts which children use most easily to grasp new knowledge.

From the outline plans here to teaching practice there is still a step to take. It is the step of finding the most vivid illustration of an incident, collecting the best resource materials, deciding what tasks to give the children, considering what questions can help them appreciate something more fully, choosing helpful analogies for events and incidents, and so on. There are many books about this level of preparing for teaching practice, and school staff rooms and teachers' conferences are rich in lore for assisting with this aspect of teaching. The contribution of this book is limited to what seems to me the crucial task of selecting and organizing topics. Clearly this overlaps with the level mentioned above, and properly should provide the plan which those tasks fill out and make more precise.

As with any new model, on first acquaintance it may seem complicated. This is due in part at least to its being different from what we are accustomed to. After so much exposure and the almost universal assertion that we must begin units and lessons by stating objectives, the presently dominant model can come to seem "natural." This alternative model, which nowhere mentions objectives, is, I hope it is clear, based on principles which are certainly no less sound and possibly much more sound than those on which the objectives—content—methods—evaluation model rests. After some practice using it I think it will be found to be a much more "natural" way to approach planning teaching. I hope the examples I have given in this chapter show how it can be used and that its use encourages more educationally valuable teaching. I hope, also, that it can be seen how it encourages teaching which is likely to be routinely meaningful and engaging to children.

CHAPTER 4

The Story Form Across the Curriculum

INTRODUCTION

It may appear plausible that the story form can be useful in organizing content that is made up mainly of events, people, and affective meaning. Those are, after all, the crucial components of fictional stories. So areas such as history and social studies readily lend themselves to story-form organization. But I have claimed that the principles developed in the first two chapters are also relevant to other curriculum areas, even mathematics. In this chapter I will try to support that claim.

The principles of the first two chapters concern what children find meaningful and engaging. The general conclusion is that if we focus on children's imaginative activity, we can see a range of sophisticated and powerful conceptual tools in use. Those tools need not be restricted to what we normally consider imaginative activities, as in fine arts, fantasy, and so on. The pedagogical task is to work out how we can organize content about the real world in such a way as to encourage ordinary children to use their considerable intellectual abilities in learning. I have exemplified the story-form model so far by means of social studies and history content. But the task now is not so much fitting the model to mathematics, language arts, and science, as reconceiving those areas in terms of the principles embodied in the model. Thus, how we teach cannot be considered a merely technical matter cut off from questions about what we teach. (By "reconceiving" curriculum areas, I do not mean that we should make them subservient to how we learn about them, but rather that we can organize them in ways that are both true to the epistemological nature of the discipline and more accessible to children. The kind of reconceiving I mean will be evident in the following examples.)

We tend to think of mathematics as a set of computational strategies organized for teaching purposes in a hierarchy of difficulty in a rather loose logical sequence. If we reconceive mathematics in terms of the educational principles of the earlier chapters. we come to see it rather differently. The computational tasks remain central, but instead of seeing mathematics simply as the sequence of computational tasks we begin to see them in a context. Seeing mathematics as computational tasks is a result of abstracting them from the human context in which they were invented for human purposes. What re-emerges when we consider mathematics from the perspective of the principles developed earlier is precisely that suppressed human context.

In this chapter, then, I will explore what it might mean for mathematics teaching, and for language arts, and science teaching, to reconceive them in the human contexts which can make them most meaningful and engaging. I will then outline how one might plan a unit or lesson in each area using the story-form model. Because the principles have implications for curriculum as well as for planning teaching, I will briefly discuss the ways that, it seems to me, we are driven to reconceive those subjects for pedagogical purposes. These discussions will precede the examples in each section. But the implications for curriculum go further than I can indicate in a brief discussion of particular disciplines. Indeed, it should not be inferred that because I try to exemplify the model in a set of discrete traditional curriculum areas like science, mathematics, language arts, and social studies that these principles lead us to a curriculum broken up in this way. In order to address this issue I will have a concluding chapter on implications for the curriculum. As this is intended primarily as a book on planning teaching, I will restrict my comments in the following chapter to sketching the kind of overall elementary curriculum structure that seems to me to follow from the principles and model developed earlier.

SOCIAL STUDIES

Perhaps least needs to be said about social studies, at least in terms of exemplifying the story-form model. The two examples in the previous chapter suggest ways in which social studies and historical material can be shaped by the model. In that shaping there is no need to falsify anything; rather it is a means of exposing an important level of meaning to which children can have ready access.

The content of social studies involves events, values, places, intentions, individual people and groups — all the material out of which fictional stories are composed. Thus it may seem more easy or obvious to be able to use this model to organize such material. The content of social studies, it may be felt, already comes partly story-shaped. There is a sense in which this is true, of course. But, equally, I think one can be misled by the seeming ease with which one can use this model in social studies. The danger is that one might be tempted by this relative easiness to slot content into the various categories of the model without thinking about what is really important in a topic and exposing *that* in terms of telling binary opposites. I suppose my fear is that the area to which the model might initially have some direct appeal is also the area in which it can most easily be abused; becoming in its turn a new mechanical planning device.

The principles developed earlier led me to suggest that the conventional way of presenting social studies material in the elementary classroom is quite as much at odds with the model as is the conventional way of presenting mathematics. The fact that the content of elementary social studies includes people — indeed, children themselves and their families — more or less familiar environments, events, and so on, does not by itself make the subject readily accessible and meaningful to children. Indeed such content can very easily appear no less "abstracted" than numbers. The pedagogical point, however, is with meaning and imaginative engagement. It is precisely these that make the elementary social studies curriculum problematical in terms of this model. Who we are, what a community is, and so on, are things we learn by slow experience; it is immensely difficult to expose for young children the importance of these in conceptual terms. They live their importance. An irony of this argument, which I will return to in the conclusion to this chapter, is that the curriculum area which seems most accommodating to this model, is one which the principles on which the model is based implies should be abolished.

Even so, let us apply the model to rather different social studies content than was considered earlier. In this example I will try to show how the principles behind this model can help to make accessible and meaningful content that is usually considered too difficult for children. Let us see what the model might produce in the way of a unit on Communism and Capitalism for nine or ten year olds.

1.   **Identifying importance:**
     What is most important about this topic?
     Why should it matter to children?
     What is affectively engaging about it?

The conflict between capitalism and communism is one of the major "stories" of the modern world. A huge range of political and economic events are interpreted in terms of it. It matters because these two major systems embody different values, and an understanding of their different aims, hopes, and beliefs is important to understanding much of what is going on in the world today. It matters also, of course, because the conflict of these systems may kill us. Any hope of preventing such an outcome of their armed mutual suspicion and hostility must begin in some mutual understanding. This conflict is affectively engaging because it represents an ongoing story of the battle between prominent values — values which constantly play a part in our everyday dealings within our social environment, and within families.

2.   **Finding binary opposites:**
     What powerful binary opposites best catch
     the importance of the topic?

In dealing with the higher age levels in the elementary school we might replace binary "opposites" with binary "pairs." The more simple dramatic oppositions can begin to give way to somewhat more sophisticated binary structuring of content. We could, of course, present communism and capitalism as opposites in some significant ways. This is, after all, how politicians on both sides tend to represent these political and economic systems. We hear of "evil empires" and "imperialist aggressors" and so on, apparently without end. That is, the usual form in which these two complex systems are expressed, and apparently conceptualized, by press and politicians is as fairly simple variants on those most basic binary opposites, good/bad. This seems common to both sides, only the specification of which side represents good and which bad changes. If our purpose is education, this pair will not do.

What concepts children can grasp readily, and grasp readily with, can expose something profound about communist and capitalist systems, and provide also the binary structure between which the topic can be organized? Let us take equality/freedom as our binary pair. By such a choice we will show the conflict between capitalist and communist systems as based upon a different set of values informing them. Or rather, not so much a different set as a different order of priority among values that they both share. In this case we will focus on freedom and equality. Both systems consider these important, but capitalism places higher value on freedom than on equality, and communism places higher value on equality than on freedom.

In organizing the content of the unit, we will show that this conflict about value priorities influences all aspects of the two systems, how they are organized and why they come into conflict. As is always the case with this model, we begin with concepts that children already profoundly understand. They may not, of course, be able to give definitions of "equality" or "freedom," but they know them from their experience in families, in groups and gangs, and so on. So we will not teach those concepts. We may, however, need to exemplify them in easily recognizable scenarios from daily life. A function of the unit then is to make these concepts more sophisticated by showing the content of the unit in terms of them.

As I have noted before, the choice of binary opposites or pairs in this model is the crucial act. It is here that the hard thinking has to go on. Needless to say, I have not chosen freedom/equality casually, but because I think this pair gets at something important and profoundly true, and so one can expose by means of them that importance and truth to children.

3. **Organizing content into story form:**
    **3.1   What content most dramatically embodies
          the binary pairs, in order to provide
          access to the topic?**

In our opening lesson we must show dramatically the differences that result from holding "freedom" as a more important social value than "equality" and vice versa. We might look for an incident where communist and capitalist countries clash in a way that exposes precisely the different value priorities that are to form our organizing props. Or one might begin with a description of a country in which transportation is free, but in which you need official permission to go anywhere, and consider that in contrast to a country where you are free to go wherever you like, but transportation costs a lot of money.

But we need quickly to move to a way of showing that different value priorities lead to different social arrangements. A simple introduction to this might be to consider the differences in the way a school or classroom might be organized if we hold freedom more important than equality, and vice versa. In the free classroom, people do not have to work if they do not want to; they can play, talk, whatever. We will see greater diversity in such a system and, if there are examinations at the end of the year, greater "inequality" in the results. We will find, too, that the freedom of choice of some will impinge on the choices of others. At this point we will see the call for some principle of equality putting a constraint on unlimited freedom. In the "equal" classroom we will find more conformity, more rules, and more sanctions to support the rules. If we are to preserve equality as far as possible than clearly we cannot let everyone do what they want. But we will see also that an exclusive stress on equality leads to absolute conformity and suppression of individual differences. Some degree of freedom might be seen as a necessary constraint on unlimited equality.

The potential problem with this opening, however, is that the school in capitalist societies is intended to be an important agent of equality's constraint on freedom. In general, in capitalist societies equality is only "of opportunity," not of achievement or enjoyments of the benefits available in society. "Free enterprise" is the freedom to use one's enterprise to make oneself as unequal as possible, while not impinging too greatly on others' freedom.

Alternatively, the teacher might construct — or use a publisher's version of — a simulation game based on the "shipwrecked-on-an-island" theme. The class would be divided into two. Each group would be given an identical map of the island and a list of its resources, along with an understanding that rescue is impossible for at least three years. There will be adequate supplies of food and material for shelter, clothing, etc. if the group is adequately organized for gathering, fishing, cultivating, and so on. Each group's instructions, however, contain rules they must follow in organizing themselves. Each group has to make survival a paramount value, but thereafter one group must arrange for as much individual freedom as possible and the other for as much equality as possible. The instructions will encourage the groups to develop differences in their social arrangements that echo those found in capitalist and communist countries. The degree of leading instructions will be determined by the age and ability of the class.

Another alternative, using a guided role-play adapted fi m Kehoe's (1984) model, would be to divide the class into t' ree groups. Arrange the class so that group A sits to one side, group B to the other, and C in the middle (following the example in Diagram 1). Group C have cards on which there are a set of questions and groups A and B have answers to those questions. The questions and answers are numbered. Question 1, for example, will have an answer 1 in group A and an

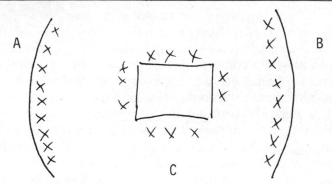

Diagram 1: *Classroom arrangement for guided role-playing*

---

answer 1 in group B. A's and B's answers will be different. There might be a question and answers such as the following:

C. Q. 7.   "What should be my attitude to money?"

A. A. 7.   "You should try to get as much money as possible. The more money you have the more goods you can buy and the more fun you can have. Also you get money by doing things that are good for other people. So the more money you get the more you are helping others as well as yourself."

B. A. 7   "Money is not very important. You should only want as much money as is necessary for your food, clothing, housing, and basics like that. Everyone should receive about the same amount of money regardless of what job they do, so that everyone can get about the same amount of goods. Trying to get more money than someone else is bad."

The students in group C are given about twenty question cards to distribute among themselves, and the students in groups A and B distribute among themselves an equal number of answer cards. The students are encouraged in asking and answering the questions to stick to the meaning on the card, but to put that meaning in their own words and to try to be as persuasive as possible. In some cases the A answers will seem more attractive, and in some cases B's will have more appeal to average children. In some cases the social results of stressing equality are more attractive and in some cases the social results of stressing freedom will seem more desirable. (C. Q. "Should I be allowed to think and say whatever I like?")

After ten questions and answers, the children in group C can be asked whether they would prefer to live in group A's country or group B's. The teacher could ask them why they choose one or the other, or why they might be ambivalent. After the twenty questions and answers are completed, the C children can be asked to vote which country they will join, and then the whole class can be asked what they think are the good points and bad points about the two countries. Then, depending on the sophistication of the class, the teacher might ask which countries they think A and B represent. Perhaps the U.S.S.R. and U.S.A. will be identified after some discussion, which might need more or less guidance. The teacher can then ask who C is. C can be considered a Third World country looking at the pros and cons of capitalism and communism, caught between what seem like competing attractions, but attractions that also carry inseparable negative features as well.

Well, these are some alternative ways of trying to establish in a dramatic way some of the social differences that follow from holding equality or freedom as the higher ideal. No doubt experienced teachers might be able to come up with many better alternatives. The point of the opening, however, is to establish clearly the importance of our binary structuring concepts, and establishing them prominently and clearly so that we can use them to attach the rest of the content of our unit to.

3.2 What content best articulates the topic into a developing story form?

Our binary concepts provide us with criteria for selecting the content of the rest of our unit. We will look at, say, the U.S.A. through the concept of freedom. That is, we will focus on those aspects of social life, and history, that most clearly show the high value put upon freedom. This might begin with the American Revolution, and consider the Civil War. Of course, there was much else besides the desire to promote freedom involved in these events, but our focus is on the way in which the high value placed on freedom played a genuine and important role in these events. Again, this involves simplification not falsification. Similarly, we might consider the fact that the newspapers often abuse politicians and are free to publish almost anything they wish — unless it infringes on the freedom of others. Enormous diversity of beliefs and styles of living are protected by the laws. Business life encourages "free enterprise," regulating the growth and operations of business as little as is felt necessary to protect the freedom of the people against the power of growing businesses. That is, we would select elements of life in capitalist countries that exemplify the high value placed on freedom. We would, perfectly properly, see the most general structure of these societies as powerfully influenced by their commitment to freedom.

These lessons might be taught along with a related set on social life in the U.S.S.R. and how it is as powerfully influenced by the commitment to equality. We might consider the role of women, the free access to social services that are not free in the U.S.A., and so on. Or one might combine the two perspectives around particular themes; taking the press, for example, and considering its role in a society committed most intensely to freedom and in a society similarly committed to equality.

The main purpose of the body of the unit is to show how the ideal influences the society. We will want to show all those aspects of the U.S.A. that most powerfully show its belief in the value of freedom as a social good, epitomized in the Statue of Liberty. In our view of the U.S.S.R. we will, again, focus on its ideal, and show those areas where the state takes from each according to ability, and provides for each according to need.

4. Conclusion:
   **What is the best way of resolving the dramatic
   conflict inherent in the binary opposites?
   What degree of mediation of those opposites
   is it appropriate to seek?**

We might conclude our unit over a number of lessons. Our educational purpose is to provide some form of mediation between the two ideals presented earlier; a task complicated by the need also to provide some mediation between the simple-minded rhetoric which is common from media and politicians. There are a number of ways we might go about such mediation.

We might, for example, spend some time considering the difficulties in achieving either ideal, and also the difficulties that follow from the two systems seeing themselves in competition. This latter tends to make each system more insistent on the higher value of its ideal, and so both less able to see the value of the other and also more likely to give less weight to the alternative value.

Unconstrained freedom leads to great freedom for the few and an inability of the many to exercise their legal and theoretical freedoms. We might, to exemplify this, consider the distribution of money in capitalist societies, and consider what happens when so many freedoms are available only if one can pay for them. The product of an excessive instantiation of freedom is a privileged few and a poor, uneducated, less healthy many. This point might be made clear by a continuation of the desert island game, by ensuring an unequal distribution of money on the "freedom" island. We might mediate further by then focusing on the agencies in capitalist countries that try to promote equality against the excesses of freedom — "freedom for whom to do what?" might be a key phrase. So we might consider the social role of the school as a constraint on unfettered freedom — but what about private schools? Or on the law and central or federal governments — but do they interfere too much?

Similarly, we need to consider unrestrained equality. This leads easily to grim conformity and repression, because only by repression of all signs of individual differences can the most extreme notion of equality be instantiated. We can exemplify this by considering the controls on movement, on family life, on work, on speech and thought, in communist countries. We can mediate further by considering those agencies in communist societies that defend against excessive equality — the law, focusing especially on those elements that protect the individual's rights, the school, and the central government.

That is, one of the slight ironies that may be a product of our mediation, is that the same institutions tend to serve in the different systems as a defence against the extreme imposition of the one ideal and the suppression of the influences of the other. (It might be instructive to consider the Soviet education system as one of the most élitist in the world, and the American progressivist system as one of the most socialist.)

We might also conclude our mediation by considering the failures of both systems to achieve their ideals, and the abuses that ignoring the other's ideal lead to. We would thus be focused onto the dachas and the palatial holiday villas of the party élite in the U.S.S.R., the special stores inaccessible to the ordinary citizen, the refusal to allow Jewish emigration to Israel, and so on. We will, that is, focus on the variety of abuses that follow from the refusal to acknowledge in one's social system the human value of freedom. Equivalently, we will be focused on racism as an expression of the refusal to acknowledge the human value of equality. Class-systems, in which the large lowest class lacks adequate access to good quality health care, education, steady employment, and the necessities of dignified life, are the inevitable product of valuing freedom and slighting equality. If "freedom for whom to do what?" is one key phrase, its counterpart can be "all people are equal, but some are more equal than others."

5.   Evaluation:
     How can we know whether the topic has been
     understood, its importance grasped, and
     the content learned?

Children's learning of much of the content of the two systems could be assessed from traditional evaluation procedures. The importance of this topic involves seeing not just how certain values undergird social and political systems but also that the two major systems in the world are in conflict in part due to their differently valuing two important human ideals. This conflict is exacerbated by politicians who seem unable to understand that the "other side" is not made up of villains who are failing to uphold the rightful valuation of the ideal of freedom or of equality, but are fallible people attempting to build systems based on different value priorities. This understanding can be evaluated only imprecisely from discussions and students' ways of dealing with tasks related to the issue. If children persist in talking and writing the way most politicians continue to do, we can be sure that we have failed. The typical political rhetoric in both systems is of a level that a society committed to education would not tolerate in nine year olds.

As an appendix to this example, I should note that I am aware that such a unit as this might cause trouble with some parents and some groups in communities east and west. It is, I realize, a dangerous topic to choose to exemplify a teaching technique; dangerous because there may be some who will think my characterization of one or both systems wildly inaccurate or inappropriate. My point here, however, is not to advocate such a unit for nine-year-olds. Indeed, I think this content is more useful taught later, for reasons I have given elsewhere (Egan, 1979). My point is to show how the story-form model can help to make accessible and meaningful a kind of social studies content that is normally considered beyond pre-teenagers. Even if readers think I am representing communism and/or capitalism inappropriately, I hope they will concentrate on how the model works in organizing this complex and important content into a form that makes it accessible to children without trivializing it. The key is to structure the unit on powerful binary concepts and then consistently illustrate and elaborate these concepts with the content of the unit. The educational purpose of this unit is to show that holding different value priorities leads to different social structures — not to argue that one is better or worse than the other. (A commercially produced unit along these lines that could be used in the U.S.S.R. and in western capitalist countries would surely contribute to mutual understanding and to children's education. The difficulties such a unit would have in practice is an index of how deeply flawed are both system's attempts to achieve their ideals.)

MATHEMATICS

Using the story-form model in the elementary school will influence the curriculum towards greater coherence. I will try to illustrate this in the next chapter, but the central reason why this is so will become evident in this brief look at the use of the model in mathematics. The tendency towards greater coherence or interconnectedness among elements of the curriculum is in part a result of the constant focus on, and use of, the set of powerful underlying concepts children have available for learning. By tying whatever content that is to be made meaningful to the set of underlying concepts one necessarily generates, or reflects, connections among the range of human experiences and knowledge that form the curriculum. By focusing on the surface content, as is so common, we reflect only differences, and represent mathematics, social studies, science, and language arts as distinct and largely unconnected realms. Recommendations for inter-disciplinary or integrated studies, or projects drawing on many areas of knowledge, are attempts to make connections across disciplines. These schemes are usually based on establishing connections at the level of content — using mathematics problems in a social studies unit, for example. The nature of the connections established by applying the story-form model is rather different, but leads I think to a more profound sense of coherence.

Mathematics in the elementary school curriculum is usually seen as a set of computational skills that have to be mastered. One of the influences of progressivism was to try to reduce the abstraction of mathematics by relating computational tasks to the experience of the child. This was taken even further in the social efficiency movement. The progressivist idea was to make the computations meaningful to the child by relating them to real problems and activities in the child's environment. The mathematics curriculum became increasingly shaped by considerations of what mathematical skills children needed in their daily lives and would need to be effective citizens. So we saw in the earlier part of this century those reforms which are now taken for granted in the mathematics curriculum. Particular mathematical skills are justified largely in terms of their social utility and the methods of instruction lean heavily towards "real-life" problems. There is thus a considerable emphasis on computations involving money, and size, quantity, volume, proportion, and fractions related to the purchase of goods or cooking or whatever seems related to the children's present or future roles. The contribution of neo-progressives, particularly through Piaget's work, is to add concrete activities as a preliminary to mastery of these basic mathematical skills.

This movement represented an important attempt to "humanize" a mathematics curriculum that had been seen as too abstract — abstracted, that is, from anything meaningful in the child's experience. The impulse towards "humanization" seems to me valuable, but in the case of the progressivist moves it was an impulse tied up with the *ad hoc* principles criticized in Chapter One. As Dewey himself observed, many progressivist reforms seemed to involve a clearer vision of what was wrong with traditional practices than of what might adequately replace them.

Does the story-form model provide an alternative means of "humanizing" the mathematics curriculum? As the progressivists observed, the problem with mathematics from the perspective of so many children is its abstraction from human intentions and emotions. This abstraction, however, is not something that is, whether we like it or not, just true about the nature of mathematics. Mathematics is not an inhuman activity. People made it for human purposes. The key to humanizing it, or, better, rehumanizing it for children is to tie the computational tasks back to the human intentions, hopes, fears, etc. that generated them in the first place. If children can see a particular mathematical computation not simply as a dehumanized skill to be mastered but rather as a particular solution to a particular human hope, intention, fear, or whatever, then we can embed the skill in a context that is meaningful.

This may seem a somewhat roundabout way of making

a point about the elementary mathematics curriculum. I want to stress, though, that the effect of using the story-form model is to re-embed particular mathematical computations in the human contexts in which they properly belong. And perhaps I might add that the pride that was involved in abstracting mathematics from its human contexts is itself motivated by comprehensible human purposes. The aim of a mathematics curriculum derived from the principles embodied in the story-form model is not to humanize mathematics in the essentially trivial way common in progressivism. It is not a matter of trying to reduce the abstraction of the computations. The point is to ensure that children can indeed more successfully use and understand the abstract computations. The abstractness, to say it again, is not the problem; it is the dehumanization that is the problem.

All very fine, but how do you teach counting by means of the story-form model? Let us see what we come up with if we apply the model to the most basic of mathematical skills. Our lesson will assume that children have learned the simple integers and we want to introduce 10s and 100s, giving an understanding of the decimal system.

1. **Identifying importance:**
   What is most important about this topic?
   Why should it matter to children?
   What is affectively engaging about it?

What is important is that children understand the ingenuity of our decimal system. We will want to convey this as something wonderful, almost magic. To the early Greeks, to Pythagoras, for example, numbers were imbued with magic. He travelled to Egypt to learn from the priests. For counting and the decimal system to be engaging, some element of this magic, this wonder at the ingenuity of basic mathematical inventions, must come across.

2. **Finding binary opposites:**
   What powerful binary opposites best catch
   the importance of the topic?

As our concern is to convey the ingenuity and wonder of the decimal system, we might choose the binary opposites of ingenuity and cluelessness.

3.   Organizing content into story form:
    3.1   **What content most dramatically embodies the binary opposites, in order to provide access to the topic?**

Our purpose is to expose the wonder and ingenuity of counting. Our first task then is to show that what we take for granted, what is such a casual routine these days, is a product of amazing achievements. We need to make clear to children, and to remind ourselves, that there is a profoundly important distinction between our number sense and counting. Our number sense is intuitive, but counting is learned. A number of species share with us a number sense, but only humans have invented elaborate tricks for counting.

We might explain this to children by telling the story of the crow that was eating the farmer's grain. The farmer decided to shoot the crow. It had made its nest in his barn. But whenever the farmer approached the barn the crow flew away. When he left the barn, the crow flew back. Thinking to trick the crow, the farmer took a friend with him to the barn. The farmer stayed in the barn when the friend left. But the crow was not fooled, and stayed in his tree until the farmer came out too. The next day the farmer took two friends with him to the barn, and he stayed behind when the two friends left. But still the crow waited till he came out before returning to its nest. The next day the farmer took three friends, with the same result. Next he took four, and then five friends. When the five came out, the farmer remaining behind, the crow flew back to its nest, and the farmer shot it.

The crow's number sense is about as good as a human being's. It cannot distinguish precisely once numbers reach about five or six. Some species do much better. There is a species of wasp, *Genus Eumenus*, in which the female is much bigger than the male. The mother can sense which grub will produce a female and which a male. The mother provides five bugs for each hatching male grub and ten for each female (Dantzig, 1967).

There are some languages that have words for every color in the rainbow, but no word for color. Some have many number words, but no word for number. In the Thimshian language there are number words for flat objects and animals, and different number words for round objects and time, and yet other number words for counting people, others for canoes, and so on. Also it is not obvious that what two apples and two turnips and two canoes have in common is twoness. That particular abstraction is not one our attention is drawn to if our interest is in the function of apples, turnips, or canoes. The focus on this level of abstract counting is a relatively recent interest. Its recentness is in part indicated by how many different words we have for referring to two of different things: pair, brace, couple, twin, and so on.

The point of these examples is to draw attention to our tendency to take for granted certain concepts that have taken millenia to develop, especially when they have become embedded in our language conventions. They are not at all as obvious as we tend to assume, and we need to be sensitive to the fact that they are not as obvious to children as they have come to seem to us. I suppose we might call this the problem of adult egocentrism — a kind that seems analogous to the egocentrism Piagetians attribute to children.

We might for the opening articulation of our binary opposites restrict ourselves to telling the story of the crow and the farmer and then going on to demonstrate the distinction between number sense and counting. The teacher might take two or three marbles in her hands and quickly open and close them in front of the class, asking "How many marbles are there here?" All children will be able to tell. Then she might try the same thing with eight or nine marbles. Some children will guess the right number, some the wrong number. Perhaps then increase the number of marbles to fourteen. Then let the children count the marbles. The teacher can explain that we are just like the crow in our number sense, but different in that we can count. The farmer's and our ingenuity is what makes the difference between our and the crow's number sense, and our ability to count.

3.2   What content best articulates the topic into a developing story form?

We want now to expose something of the cleverness of counting that is involved in the decimal system. If we enter a classroom and all the chairs are full and some children are standing, we can tell immediately that there are more children than chairs. Or, if there are some empty chairs, that there are more chairs than children. The teacher can use the marbles and cups or blocks to show this in a simple way. The children can then be told that this was how nearly all counting used to be done. It was not by means of abstract counting, but by matching things with the objects to be counted. Some people would make a cut in a stick to represent each object, or drop a pebble in a pot. The Latin for a cut is *talea*, leading to "tally," and for a pebble is *calculus*, leading to "calculus."

The trouble with these is dealing with very large numbers. Counting lots and lots of cuts or pebbles becomes eventually as confusing as counting the things they represent. Let us pose the problem faced in reality by a king in Madagascar long ago. He wanted to know how many soldiers he had in his army. We can invent for him one ingenious counsellor and five clueless counsellors. The army was gathered together on a wide plain. These people did not have complicated ways of counting, and would need to use some matching method. How could they count the milling groups of soldiers? The five clueless counsellors wandered ineffectually to and fro, each having to confess failure. It was a bare plain with nothing to match against the soldiers. The king turned to the ingenious counsellor, who came up with a solution.

The ingenious counsellor had the five clueless counsellors look around till they had each found ten small pebbles. He then had them stand in a line beside a narrow space between two rocks at the side of the plain where the army was gathered. A table was put in front of them and a bowl in front of each clueless counsellor. The army was then ordered to march one by one between the rocks. As each soldier went by, the first counsellor put one pebble into his bowl. Once he had counted ten, he picked up the ten pebbles again. Each time he picked up the ten pebbles, the counsellor next to him put one pebble into his bowl. So after ten soldiers went by there were no pebbles in the first bowl and one in the second. When the first counsellor had picked up his set of pebbles ten times there were ten stones in the second counsellor's bowl. Similarly, once all his ten pebbles were down he picked them up again. As he picked them up, the third counsellor put one pebble into his bowl. After the third counsellor had put down all his pebbles and picked them up, the fourth counsellor put one of his pebbles into his bowl. And so on.

And so they went on through the morning as the soldiers trooped rapidly between the stones. After some hours they had all passed through. The fifth counsellor had 1 pebble in his bowl, the fourth 3, the third 8, the second 6 and the first 7. So there were exactly 13,867 soldiers in the army. By ingenuity the king's clever counsellor had counted the whole army with just fifty pebbles. The teacher could let two children with marbles count the class this way, or a group could count beeps generated by a computer, or whatever the teachers' ingenuity might suggest.

Depending on the teacher's assessment of how well the principle has been grasped, she might either move on to the conclusion or introduce another example of ingenuity solving a problem in a way that shows the use of the decimal system.

4. Conclusion:
    What is the best way of resolving the dramatic conflict inherent in the binary opposites?
    What degree of mediation of those opposites is it appropriate to seek?

The teacher might move towards a conclusion by asking the children how the king's counsellors might have counted the army if there had been no pebbles around. What have we got ten of that are easily accessible? The teacher could lead to the solution that the counsellors could have stood in line raising fingers and closing their fists on reaching ten, at which the next counsellor raised one finger, and so on. We can thus show how ingenuity enables us to use the matching system and our fingers to count up to very large numbers. The teacher can point out that it is because we have ten fingers that we use a decimal system. Until a couple of hundred years ago mathematical texts all included various finger counting methods. Children might have fun learning some of the simpler methods.

The conclusion should stress the ingenuity of our basic numbering system. The task for the teacher is in large part to make wonderful what has become routine. Or rather, to recover what wonders underlie the routine. Children are encouraged to admire the ingenuity of the clever counsellor, of course, but some mediation might follow from the recognition that most of us are clueless. But yet, the wonder is that even those of us who are most clueless can get some sense of the ingenuity of the inventors of our counting systems as we learn them. It might be appropriate as a closing story to tell about Euclid and his 13 books of the *Elements* of mathematics. They remained the most important introduction to mathematics for 2000 years, and only after all that time were some of the cleverest people able to show how Euclid was wrong in just a few cases, or had got a few things confused. Mathematics is ingenious ways of using numbers and counting. The way the army could be counted by five people using their fingers is an example of how mathematics helps us to do difficult things quite easily. All our science and technology depends on similar ingenious counting tricks. We need to convey that mathematics is wonderful and fun. Magic number cards and tricks and games can all be useful supplements to this feeling for the wonder of mathematics. More time might be given over to such things than seems common at present.

5. Evaluation:
   How can one know whether the topic has been understood, its importance grasped, and the content learned?

There are a range of standard tests which can show whether the basic concept of placement in the decimal system has been mastered. What is more difficult to evaluate is whether or to what degree the magic of numbers has been felt by individual children. While relatively simple tests can provide indices of the degree of basic skill mastery, the teacher's sensitivity needs to come into play to sense whether children's wonder has been stimulated. As this engagement of wonder is most important early on most of the teacher's effort might wisely go on this.

In the context of the day-to-day work of the classroom teacher, it might seem a bit idle for someone sitting in his study looking out over the winter garden to write what might seem like nonsense about the magic of number — especially when it is such an uphill struggle to give so many children basic mastery over the simplest computations. But, study and winter garden notwithstanding, I am calling attention to the easier practical path, not to a lunatic theory. If the child gets a sense of wonder, then the computational skills will follow. The basic skills are incidental; what is important for mathematics learning is the magic Pythagoras felt. And in addition to magic, and connected with it, is the fun of numbers. They work like a conjuring trick. So games and tricks with numbers are one of the ways to the sense of wonder. If the magic cannot be fully attained except by the rare individual, at least the fun can be perceived by nearly all. Nearly all children have superabundant intellectual capacities to be able easily to master basic mathematical computations. The pedagogical trick is to show them why they should be interested enough to expend the intellectual energy to do so.

ENGLISH/LANGUAGE ARTS

Here, in addition to discussing the use of the story-form model, I should also say something about the fictional story. Throughout I have been distinguishing between the story-form model, which has been built from just a few basic features of the story, and the fictional story itself. It will perhaps be obvious that I think stories — ordinary fictional stories such as fairy-tales, adventures, fantasy, and dungeons and dragons style narrative explorations — have considerable educational uses. The story is not a cultural universal for nothing. The power of good stories to engage children and stimulate their imaginations, and enlarge their experience, sympathies, and understanding, is ignored at considerable educational cost. Some parents and some teachers read stories to children every day. This seems to me to have clear educational advantages.

One can list a range of educational advantages that follow a sensible program of daily story reading. Janet Kendall (1985) has argued for the following:

- it provides at its simplest a model of reading activity for children. The process of making symbols into words, and even stumbling in reading, provide a model that children are encouraged to follow;
- it expands vocabulary and thereby the range of understanding;
- it enlarges the range of concepts children can use, and thereby their knowledge about the world;
- differences between written and spoken language are made clear, as is the power of considered formal language to go beyond what is normal in everyday speech;
- it conveys the simple message that reading is important. It shows children that books can contain wonders and that the life of the mind that they stimulate can be intoxicating and ecstatic.

The routine listening to stories, then, can stimulate a whole range of cognitive skills. Children, in coming to make sense of increasingly sophisticated stories, come of necessity to develop an increasingly subtle sense of causality. They learn problem-solving, and the forming and reforming of hypotheses in the light of further knowledge. They become familiar with an increasingly wide range of human emotions and ways of responding to them: a good story will stimulate sympathy and actively develop the emotional life. They serve, in Ted Hughes' words, as "little factories of understanding. New revelations of meaning open out of their images and patterns continuously" (Hughes, 1977, p. 12).

So while the fictional story is not the subject of this essay, I can add my voice to those who appeal for an increase in the time spent by parents and teachers telling or reading stories to children. (In passing I might note the odd increase in engagement children often show in a story told in one's own words and "voice," over the fluent reading of the same story. Story-telling rather than story-reading takes a bit of practice, but is perhaps worth the effort.)

The "skills" of literacy that are considered central to the language arts curriculum are often taught and reinforced by lists of exercises. The principles of the early chapters suggest that we might call on the story-form model for such tasks — though with no guarantee that our conception of the central tasks will remain untouched. I mentioned in Chapter Three that while the story is the paradigm of the sense-making model I am building on, there are other forms that also embody some of the same basic structural features. Two of the more obvious are the game and, that miniature kind of story, the joke. Whatever particular skill one is trying to inculcate can benefit from being presented in the context of a game, joke, or puzzle — or, of course, story. This is not recommended simply as a motivational device. The point about games, jokes, and puzzles is that they embody some of the same sense-making principles common also to the story. The game, joke, or puzzle, to be educationally effective, however, should be used according to the principles laid out in Chapter Three. A joke is not only funny; it is potentially another of those little factories of understanding, a place where understanding can be made or expanded.

A simple joke often involves an opposition between a normal expectation and some incongruous element. The middle elaborates the conflict, and the conclusion resolves the incongruity in an unexpected way, or in an expected way that is made weird by the incongruity introduced at the beginning. (There is nothing so dull as attempts to describe or analyse jokes.)

Perhaps I might include here a trivial example of the use of jokes rather than contextless exercises in the development of "literary skills." I do so because, by coincidence, I was just interrupted by six-year-old David who, after persuading me to put up a sign saying "Re-elect David Egan" in my study, asked whether there was a Mr. Belly-Button Monster in the phone book. He is at the stage of taking a particular delight in talking about the body, especially the "naughty bits." I in-

vited him to look, having earlier indicated the rough principles whereby dictionaries and phone books are organized.
A six-year-old might then learn to use the dictionary searching for I do not dare to inquire about what bodily-named
people.

This contrasts with what is the commoner approach
generated by stating precise objectives. This encourages
breaking down reading (or "the reading process") and
language arts into endless skills and sub-skills. David was
also given for Christmas a Dictionary Skills book. (Not by
me.) This is a forty page, attractively produced booklet,
devoted to the sub-skills whose combination constitute the
skill of dictionary use. As with so many of these up-beat
booklets, this one concludes with an award for successful
conclusion of all the exercises. Being a book about dictionary
skills, "award" is explained as in a dictionary. It reads as
follows: "*award* (- 'word) n. pl-s from Old Norse French *es*
-(from Latin *ex* - "out of") plus *warder* "to guard" something
that is given on the basis of merit, or good work done." I
don't know about you, but I can't follow how the Old Norse
and guarding lead to the definition of award. Having worked
through the booklet I'm no better able to decipher it. This is
perhaps unfair, but it illustrates only too vividly how a focus
on exercises of subskills seems to encourage meaning and
coherence to flee. And children are expected to work through
endless such worksheets and booklets, with none of the "skill
development activities" clearly showing their purpose, meaning, relationship to anything that makes much sense beyond
the isolated and artificial world of the "skill-based"
classroom. The principles of dictionary use are pretty easy to
learn, and a few brief games, jokes, and puzzles, or stories,
with clues and help where needed, can do the job, without the
laborious building up through contextless exercises of subskills. That the development of sets of sub-skills is supposed
to be implied by scientific research is a destructive illusion
which I have discussed in detail elsewhere (Egan, 1983/1984).

This is perhaps an excessive response to a particular
booklet. I go to such lengths only because the approach of the
booklet is so common in language arts instructional
materials. We can see the process of mechanistic thinking af-

fecting the name of the area even. It was usually called simply "English" — a term for all the complexity involved in learning the language and literature. From there to "language arts" and then to "communication skills" may seem to suggest more precise and attainable objectives. What the technologizing of teaching and curriculum has tended to leave behind is the point — of learning something worth skillfully communicating. Language arts seems increasingly to be viewed as acres of skills and sub-skills which constitute "basic literacy." This movement is, of course, encouraged by an outcry at appalling "literacy" achievements — as measured by tests that focus almost exclusively on "basic skills." Thus instruction has been inexorably focused on achieving the skills the tests measure, and more meaningful purposes for reading and writing become gradually suppressed. The justification for reading at the elementary school is, simply, ecstasy — the intoxication that can be achieved by stimulation and use of the imagination. If we cannot get students to experience this, then all the sub-skill mastery in the world will be a sterile achievement.

This is much the same point I made in the previous section about the wonder of mathematics. Here again it may seem an exotic point, perhaps relevant only to an élite for whom literacy is to be more than a utilitarian accomplishment. But I mean it in a most straightforward, pragmatic way, as an observation relevant to everybody because relevant to the nature of literacy. Language arts is about intellectual ecstasy. If we want children to learn to read, the most important step is to give them reasons for bothering. Learning to read is easy; nearly all children have superabundantly the capacities required for learning to read. What is too commonly lacking is any reason why they should put in the effort. Endless skills and sub-skills to be mastered for some vague utilitarian end are hardly an adequate incentive or justification for the effort required, especially for children whose home background does not provide the incentive or justification. In light of the vast industry of research on reading this might seem simple-minded. But none of the research I have seen mentions ecstasy, and this seems to me the irreducible core of what literacy is about. If this is forgotten and reading is seen as an increasingly complex technical task, to be built carefully bit by bit through the agglomeration of sets of sub-skills, I think there is little hope. We become like the scientists of Laputa — methodologically enormously sophisticated, just forgetting the point of the exercise.

Of course reading is an enormously complex phenomenon, if our concern is to describe and explain it psychologically. But that is not our educational concern. Our educational concern is the much simpler one of teaching children to do it. We know how to do this. Indeed there are lots of ways; we need only be a bit sensitive and sympathetic when particular problems are encountered. The technologizing, and pathologizing, of the classroom, seems to contribute nothing to the educational task, and indeed to detract from it by focusing attention towards the psychologist's interests in literacy rather than the educator's. There is a danger, putting it this way, of being taken for an anti-scientific know-nothing. I think rather that this way of putting it derives from an ability to tell the difference between psychological and educational concerns. There has been, it seems to me, an educationally destructive confusion of the two, largely due to the enormous, though now perhaps waning, influence of psychology over education.

A similar point needs to be made about writing. Too close a focus on skills and sub-skills as constituting writing again misses the point that the educational justification for learning to write has to be seen in the ecstatic power to create and express one's own world. As with reading, one can list a range of values that come from writing and that form some justifications for learning to write:

- writing is making; it allows us to make images or events or characters. As words are used to describe real things or events, so we can use them to create things or events that do not exist.
- we can put our private sense of things into a public form. Our personal view can be put into a form which makes it public, which establishes it as itself an object in the world.
- the imagined worlds and characters can become

vehicles in carrying onward their fantasy creations.

- writing requires and encourages making practical and aesthetic judgements; it is a constructive "structure-seeking more than a rule-abiding activity" (Eisner, 1978). If writing becomes primarily a rule-abiding activity then we are undermining the intrinsic sources of satisfaction it can provide to the child. It is the structure-seeking, the pursuit of satisfactory forms, that can give deeper pleasure than following a rule. The rule is a means to the end of structure-seeking, not an end in itself.
- the made elements — characters, events, descriptions — can be formed into the greater whole of a story, or essay. Completing such a larger written structure calls into play additional abilities.
- one can structure written forms to provide persuasive images that can persuade others of the validity of the writer's private vision. These persuasive achievements can begin at a simple level of conveying the validity of how something appears to, or feels like, to the writer.
- one can create in others ideas and emotions that they would otherwise not have.
- the world can become a source of ideas, images, and characters that can become subject matter for one's writing and one's aesthetic purposes. This can sharpen the perception and enlarge sympathy for the unique.

Now if this seems like a neat list, the credit should go to Elliot W. Eisner. What I have done is take the points he makes in his article "What do children learn when they paint?" (Eisner, 1978), and convert them to writing. One might elaborate them much more richly, and I recommend that those who would be interested in doing so should read his article and consider its relevance to writing as well as painting.

The point of this list is that most of the items on it concern the satisfactions of making with words. Learning to write is learning the ecstatic power to create and express one's own world and one's own self. This may involve inventing the names of players in one's soccer or hockey team, with their scores and histories, or a dungeons and dragons map, or a fantasy story, or an imaginary friend, or the baby sister or family one lacks. It is this power and its satisfactions that provides the justification for expending the effort that learning to write requires. These may again seem like fancy theoretical terms removed from the everyday reality of the classroom, but they are I think the important things to be borne in mind when planning to teach writing. If our aim is merely some future utilitarian activities, then we are losing touch with education.

Well, so much for the extensive polemical introduction. I have run the danger of seeming to set up "skills" and the story-form model as binary opposites. I do not mean this: of course one has to acquire skills bit by bit. My point, and the reason for the apparent opposition, is that the focus on skills is taken by so many teachers, persuaded perhaps by textbooks and packaged literacy programs, as the scientific way to respond to the social pressure for increased "basic skills." This direction seems to me a radical step further towards sterility and meaning-impoverishment in elementary schools — for all the reasons given earlier.

So how should we plan a "story-form" lesson on how to use the comma to a third-grade class? The simplest answer, I suppose, is that we would never do such a thing. One would incorporate teaching the use of the comma into some more meaningful writing activity. One would point out in texts one was reading that commas are used to break up the text to make it more easy to understand, and to avoid possible confusions. One might show the children a page of medieval writing, which lacked commas. In those days people nearly always read aloud, to help interpret the sense. The comma is an important invention, helping our eyes easily to take in meaning-chunks. Learning to use commas appropriately is a long-term achievement. One would encourage children to use them, correcting cases of clear error or inappropriate use. Such "skills" are picked up incidentally: there are no hard and fast rules about comma-usage. The convention today is for far fewer commas than was the case a couple of hundred years ago. In order to clarify some basic principles of comma use one might invent simple verbal games, in which the use of the comma affects the meaning. You are at a party and can choose the content of your loot-bag by putting commas in the appropriate places: paper pencils candy planes chocolate dolls truck stickers. Or one can provide brief stories or jokes whose meaning is changed by changing the place of the commas. These might be brief activities if the teacher thinks they might be useful. But, in general, the story-form model would lead one to see comma use as an incidental to be learned during more meaningful writing activities.

The story-form model, then, does not just lead us to teach the same things in a somewhat different way, but also leads us to teach somewhat different things. As the mechanistic objectives model tends towards those things that are more or less precisely measurable, so in language arts the tendency is to write as objectives those skills whose mastery may be relatively easily assessed. But with the story-form model, starting with the question about what is important, we are focused towards the purpose for mastery of those skills, and towards activities that justify the development of those skills, and so activities in performing which the mastery of skills becomes incidental.

What then might we teach that would be more meaningful during which — incidentally — we might teach the proper use of the comma? After pointing out the use of the comma in written material, and mentioning its purposes, and perhaps playing some simple word games or puzzles built around proper comma use, the children can be given a writing task in which they will be expected to use commas. How can the story-form model guide us in planning such a lesson?

1.   Identifying importance:

If getting the commas in the right place is an incidental, what is important about writing? Style is important, for one thing. Let us focus on that. One of the dangers in teaching writing is that our concern to convey the rules and conventions tends towards encouraging bland uniformity, or stylelessness. The writing style of most adults is a simple reflection of the conventions of their time and place. It lacks the distinctiveness that comes from learning to use the conventions and rules to express one's own individuality. What is said and written is so often nothing more than the given clichés and conventions: language masters us rather than the other way round.

So in our writing lesson we will try to teach ways of developing individual style. Learning to write is not a process wherein one can first master all the rules and conventions and then begin to be concerned about style. There is a constant tension to be played between mastery of rules and conventions and the development of individual style. This, yet again, is not some exotic and romantic theory, suitable, if it makes sense at all, for an élite few in creative writing classes. It is as important a consideration for the minority slum child as for the professional writer. To see the teaching of writing as something less than this, as a utilitarian set of sub-skills, is to strip the activity of what can make it worthwhile to learn.

Let us take a routine task for our writing lesson: the writing of a letter.

2. Finding binary opposites:

Our binary opposites are vivid individuality and dull conventionality.

3. Organizing content into story form:

3.1 The teacher might begin showing the binary opposites by reading two letters of equal length, one which is entirely conventional — with all the formulas of regards and hope-you-are-wells, the other of which is quirky, individual, and full of concrete particulars. The vividness of one and the conventionality of the other will show largely through the generality of the latter and the particularity of the former. Our opening, then, is designed to show children how the concrete particularity of their individual perception, feelings, experiences is what can best communicate vividly what is important. The teacher might take the most everyday examples, such as letters to grandma, dwelling on the affective difference between "I thought of you on my way to school this morning, grandma" and "I thought of you, grandma, as we passed the rose garden you like," or between "I hope you are well" and "I hope your back is better." Or how looking, however confusedly, for words that represent one's concrete experience and one's feeling about its particularity communicates more: Not so much "It snowed yesterday. We had a wonderful snowball fight. Tom played and Mary and I had a lot of fun," and more "I got tingly fingers throwing snowballs and got a sore throat shouting and laughing till Tom hit me in the neck and it dribbled inside my shirt." The latter is more interesting for both reader and writer.

Once the contrast between the effects of conventional abstractions and concrete particularity are established, we can proceed to the students' letter writing. If we are studying the Vikings, we might ask the students to write a letter from one of the protagonists in that unit to another. We might suggest a letter from a monk to Ivar the Boneless, trying to persuade him to leave the monasteries alone, or from Alfred to his choerls (dictated to a monk), or from Guthrum to a Viking leader in Scandinavia about Alfred, or between any characters the students may wish to have communicate. If it seems inconvenient to draw on other topics being studied, the students might like to write to their favorite character in fiction or history: Perhaps an appeal to Darth Vadar to turn from his evil ways, or to the young Abe Lincoln or Queen Elizabeth I, or whomever.

3.2 The teacher might recommend a three-part form for the letter, reflecting the general structure of the story form. First, a beginning that states the purpose for writing, second, a middle that focuses on an incident and the child's affective response to it, and third, a conclusion that draws the letter to a satisfactory close.

Some time might be spent with each of the three sections, reiterating how the purpose for writing should be expressed by focusing on concrete particularity and on experiences or incidents which best capture that individuality. Some minutes can then be allowed for writing or sketching an opening. Similarly the two remaining sections can be discussed, the principles reiterated, then time for writing in silence be allowed. The theme of these discussions must be the opposition between the conventional and general on the one hand, and vivid particularity on the other.

4. Conclusion:

As long as the children agree, drafted letters can be shared around the class, for comparisons and comment. Children can be encouraged to read what they consider to be the most vivid pieces of others' letters. They can also draw attention to remaining conventional generalities, as long as they suggest a way of improving it.

The teacher, with the children's permission, might take the letters away for editorial comments, noting errors in use of commas, amongst other grammatical rules. The next class might be spent on the children producing a final draft of their letters.

5. Evaluation:

This may take place during the class discussion of the first drafts, during the teacher's reading and editorial commenting, and after the final revisions. In the first case the teacher's sensitivity is the evaluating instrument, and results of that informal evaluation will constantly guide the number and kind of examples given, or the degree of reiteration of the principle. With the written drafts, more stable evaluations can be made of the degree of mastery of the conventions and of the vivid particularity of the writing. The important point of the lesson is that the rules and conventions of writing are aids to the purpose of communicating in vivid and individual ways. Style in writing is in large part a matter of expressing through choice of concrete details one's individual view of the world and the flavor of one's individual experience. It is not easy to evaluate the degree to which children are learning this. It is of course much easier to evaluate whether they have learned the conventions for use of the commas. But one must not let the relative ease of this seduce us into laying greater emphasis on the incidental at the expense of what is of greater importance.

SCIENCE

The general approach to elementary science involves introducing children to relatively simple forms of the basic skills of scientific methodology — careful observation, measurement, experiment, predicting consequences — and to basic knowledge derived from the various sciences. The form of the typical elementary science program — at least those which have not remained stagnant for more than a quarter century — has been significantly affected by the large-scale curriculum projects of the 1960s (such as "Science Curriculum Improvement Study," "Science - A Process Approach," "The Elementary Science Study," the Nuffield science projects, Schools Council's Science 5-13 project) and the large-scale evaluations of them undertaken in the 1970s.

The programs were on the whole contemptuous of what preceded them, and they redesigned the curricula to expose the structure of science and the activities of exploration, experiment, and inquiry. The child was to engage in the process of science, not learn its products. Every expectation was that these redesigned science programs would at last give children an introduction to what science was really about. Great pride was taken, particularly in the U.S.A., in the number of scientists involved in curriculum development: "In 1963, there were 10 Nobel laureates actively involved in school science projects, whereas, in the 25 years preceding that time, not one such distinguished scientist was so engaged" (Gatewood and Osbourn, 1963, p. 355).

The results of the evaluations were a considerable disappointment. They indicated declines in knowledge, and even more dramatic declines in interest in science. The main responses to these reports have involved moves to integrate science with other subjects, to stress the human side of science, to provide more teacher autonomy rather than expect (hopelessly) that teachers will act as passive agents of the packaged program, to allow more for individual differences and let individual interests play a more significant role in choosing topics.

The present concern is to try to find a balance between a "relevant," integrated curriculum to which science makes a relatively small and rather random contribution, and a genuine introduction to scientific methods and thinking. That is, the more interdisciplinary or integrated and "relevant" the scientific contribution becomes, the less it satisfies those who think it vital to have pure science in elementary schools. On top of this dilemma is the further disturbing finding that most elementary school teachers feel ill-equipped to teach science, whereas they generally feel well-equipped to teach reading; a finding that both reflects and responds to the "back to the basics" movement.

What, then, is implied by the story-form model and its underlying principles? In elementary schools our main task is to teach children what science is, as distinct from, say, magic. This distinction is basic to scientific inquiry and is far from obvious. We tend to forget that scentific methods took millenia to reach their present state. Our first imaginative effort has to be to work out why it took so long: what is so complicated and anti-intuitive about science that it took the greatest geniuses thousands of years to work out? And given that it required so much effort for so long why should we think it can be made meaningful to elementary school children relatively easily? Scientific understanding is made up of layers of kinds of understanding, and our task is to isolate as neatly as we can the constituent layer that can best be grasped in childhood. Trying to do this is beyond the scope of the present work, except that I will attempt a sketch of one possible conclusion in the next chapter. (But see Egan 1979/85, and in press.) The main lines of the conclusions, however, can be inferred from the principles developed earlier. Our science program will be about the human adventure that began in magic and myth and gradually, through individuals' courage, ingenuity, hopes, and so on, became science. It is a human activity concerned with what works, regardless of what people think, believe, or hope for. It begins, however, in people's hopes, beliefs, and fears, and makes sense when seen in terms of human intentions. Only very late in its development does it become disinterested inquiry.

I have discussed the puzzle as conforming with some of the structural features of the story. A form of puzzle prominent in early science programs is the experiment. Many early science programs are based on a series of simple experiments. If we are to study heat, we might, among other things, take two thermometers, poke them through round pieces of cardboard, one painted white, the other black, and rest the ends of the thermometers in the water, the black and white cardboard resting on the top of the glass. Put them on a sunny window ledge. Why does one heat up more than another? We can have experiments showing that warm air expands and rises, that some metals conduct heat better than others and better than some other materials, and so on. Such activities have an engaging quality, they help to focus children's observation, and they communicate facts about heat. If we were to design a unit on heat using the story-form model what might we do differently? Let us, then, consider how we might tell the story of heat to children.

1.   **Identifying importance:**

What is humanly important about heat? It is life-enhancing power, when we control it properly. It enables us to live comfortably, to forge metals, and drive machines, and so on.

2.   **Finding binary opposites:**

The most obvious binary opposite is cold. Our identification of heat with power to improve life, however, leads us towards an opposition such as heat as helper/heat as destroyer. Our focus from such a binary pair would be on the control of heat, and our struggles to keep this rather tricky monstrous servant doing what we want.

3.   **Organizing content into story form:**

/ 3.1   We might begin with the stories of the "hot" gods. Prometheus stole the fire Zeus wanted to keep from humans and delivered it to them. Fire in the myth represents power and knowledge. Prometheus was terribly punished by Zeus, but rescued by Hercules. The god Sol, our sun, has a bright eye which watches the world. His reckless son, Phaeton, drove Sol's fiery charriot across the sky one day but could not keep it on track and scorched the earth, burning the crops. Hephaestus (whom the Romans called Vulcan), who was ugly and lame, was clever at controlling fire in his smithy. His workshop was on a rocky island from which flames and smoke poured (giving us the word Volcano). We might include that other fiery god, Mars.

These old myths introduce and embody our important theme: Heat is a central feature in the human story; the trick is to use it wisely, control it, for human benefit. It can be used to make things or to destroy.

We might also add to our introduction the story of James Watt observing the steam coming from the kettle. What would happen if the steam could not escape? Steam takes up about 16,000 times more space than water. If we heat water till it becomes steam, can we use the pressure created?

3.2 We need to build the rest of the content of the unit on the binary opposites already selected. An experiment in the classroom or lab that shows how steam can be used to do some work needs, then, to be understood in the context of Prometheus and the power of the gods that has become ours to use wisely. It is the wider context of meanings that the story-form model constantly demands.

One section of our unit might focus on heat turning water to steam and the gradual control of this into huge engines that could drive across continents and seas. We might begin with the story of Hero of Alexandria's steam engine (approx. 100 B.C.E.), and its use in religious ceremonies. We could then follow the later European development of the steam engine through the lives and purposes of the Marquis of Worcester in the seventeenth century, through Thomas Savery, Denis Papin, Thomas Newcomer, and so on. We might constantly focus on the vivid anecdotes, such as young Humphrey Potter's desire to get out of the boring job of opening and shutting taps on Newcomer's steam engine. He wanted to get out and play, so ingeniously invented an automatic system which released him from his drudgery. This section could illustrate through experiments and diagrams in a simple way how heat on water enabled people to build the Promethean railway train.

We might also consider our great nuclear engine, the sun. Though only about 1/2,000,000,000 of its energy reaches earth, that is enough to provide energy for all the green plants that support our atmosphere and animal life. We might also consider, in contrast to the benefits of the sun, the disasters it wreaks.

Throughout the unit, we will see heat, not simply as a phenomenon whose qualities are to be learned about, but as a helper or destroyer. Incidentally to this focus, children will learn about its qualities. The control and use of heat is never, in this context, a routine and casual matter; it is precisely a constant battle best caught in the myths of Prometheus, Hephaestus, and Phaeton.

4. Conclusion:

The dramatic conflict we have exemplified between the control of heat for human benefits and its destructive potential, is not one that has been resolved. Phaeton's recklessness and ambition, and Zeus's revenge, are kept at bay only by our ingenuity. We might conclude with an introduction to the vivid modern case where the benefits are great, the threats real, and the controls ingenious. This is the truly Promethean story of nuclear power. In general terms, one can explain the incredible heat that is generated by smashing apart the smallest units of matter. In general terms, one can explain how nuclear power plants control and turn into usable power these reactions. And in general terms, with particular examples, one can explain the dangers of such power getting out of control, and of the problems of disposing of radioactive wastes that the system produces.

5. Evaluation:

As with the earlier examples, the story-form model contributes nothing much to procedures for evaluation, except underlining the difficulty of precisely evaluating what is most important. Various evaluation procedures can provide indeces of how well children will have grasped the basic concepts and learned the particular content. The degree to which they will see heat and its human uses in the context of a Promethean struggle is less amenable to precise measurement, but the more easy assessments should not be allowed to displace this.

CONCLUSION

I noted near the beginning of this chapter that social studies material seemed most easily designed into this story-form model. My claim was that the model could also be applied to other areas of the curriculum equally well. It may seem that I have succeeded, but at the cost of, as it were, social studyizing the whole curriculum — that is, making science, mathematics, and language arts merely extensions of social studies. There is a certain irony in this, as I have argued elsewhere — in "Social Studies and the Erosion of Education" (Egan, 1983b) — that we should abandon the social studies curriculum and replace it with something more educationally worthwhile. (The argument was that social studies was an early twentieth-century invention designed to homogenize and "Americanize" groups of disparate cultures who flooded into the U.S.A. Whatever we now think of that homogenization and its erosion of so many rich cultural heritages, we should recognize that we no longer have any coherent purposes for the social studies curriculum. The argument has not gone without rejoinders and attacks.) Anyway, the seeming contradiction needs to be addressed.

Two main points can be made. It was John Dewey's ideal that the "subject matter of education consists primarily of the meanings which supply content to existing social life" (Dewey, 1916/66, p. 192), and in his view social studies "are so important that they should give direction and organization to all branches of study" (Dewey, 1958, p. 183). My first point, then, may be to claim that what I am doing here is suggesting a way of realizing this ideal.

This is hardly a satisfactory answer by itself, however. The principles argued for in the first chapters conflict fairly directly with those which Dewey's followers derived from his writings. But perhaps it is fair to say that the overall ideal is shared, and differences with Dewey's progressivist followers are at the level of interpreting the ideal into particular principles.

The second point is that we do not need social studies as it is presently structured if we redesign our curriculum according to the story-form principles. We are constantly dealing with the social — i.e., human — aspects of all knowledge. What we are passing over, for reasons discussed earlier, is the *content* of children's immediate environments. But the concepts that animate those environments, and are used to make them and children's social experience meaningful, are at the heart of these principles and the curriculum they direct us towards.

The structure of such a curriculum is constantly hinted at above, but not dealt with explicitly. It is perhaps worthwhile to turn now to consider very briefly and very generally just what implications these principles have for the overall structure of the elementary school curriculum.

CHAPTER 5

The Elementary School Curriculum

INTRODUCTION

This is an essay about planning teaching not about curriculum, but as one cannot radically separate the two it seems appropriate to consider briefly just what are the main im plications that follow from these principles for the curriculum. One implication mentioned earlier was towards a more coherent or interconnected curriculum, due to the use, and stimulation, of the basic conceptual tools children have available. The purpose of this chapter is to explore the main implications that seem to follow from the principles outlined in the first two chapters.

I will begin by considering some general implications that follow from the disruption of the *ad hoc* principles that have been so influential in the past, then I will consider some particular curriculum changes suggested by the alternative principles, concluding with an overall general structure for the elementary curriculum. I will embed my comment in a brief historical context.

My aim here is not to provide a detailed new curriculum. (I am trying to do something more like that elsewhere. See Egan, in press.) Rather I want to establish the general significance of replacing the *ad hoc* principles with the alternative I have argued for. This is not some theoretical concern remote from the practical tasks of teaching and curriculum decision-making. Note how the *ad hoc* principles have had such a powerful influence over the structure and sequencing of the present curriculum. My aim, then, is at least to try to describe the overall shape of an alternative elementary curriculum based on the alternative principles and model I have outlined above. The fact that I have tried to show that the planning model can be used in a variety of curriculum areas should not be seen as my accepting that the curriculum should be organized into such discrete areas in elementary schools. I want to try to show that one could plan a distinct and coherent curriculum on the alternative principles and that it would be, even in general outline, reasonable and sensible.

SOME GENERAL IMPLICATIONS FROM THE ALTERNATIVE PRINCIPLES

Before the mid-nineteenth century, the child's mind was largely seen as a somewhat resistant organ into which content could be pressed by insistent instruction. Given this view, the main pedagogical problem was seen as discovering how one could most forcefully press the content in. The main curriculum problem was organizing the content into a logical sequence, so that it would go in, in the right order.

There have been two major ideas since then about how to organize the curriculum. The earlier of the two emerged during the second half of the nineteenth century, and was the main educational expression of the enormously powerful idea of Evolution. It was believed that the human embryo recapitulates in the mother's womb the evolutionary process of the species. The curriculum expression of this "ontogeny recapitulates phylogeny" idea (the individual follows the developmental path of the species) was "culture-epochs" schemes. These were based on the plausible idea that children could best come to understand their culture by learning about it bit by bit following the sequence in which it developed. Thus children's education would begin with the earliest ages of the earth and with the first beginnings of human culture and gradually progress through their schooling to the present day. Many forms of culture-epoch curricula were devised. The idea was most influential in Germany, and from there had a considerable impact on North America.

The second idea that posed an alternative to the logical structuring of the curriculum was most fully expressed in the writings of John Dewey. It derives from what he called the psychological method. This was the result of arguing that children's minds were not merely passive organs into which content could be pressed. On the contrary we can see that they are active, and capable of enormous and easy learning in the informal settings of everyday experience. If we attend to the ways children learn in their daily lives outside of school, we can devise ways of organizing the curriculum to enhance their learning in school. Prominent among the principles he enunciated was the need to begin a topic with students directly experiencing some aspect of it in a way that is meaningful in their lives. This led to curriculum conclusions such as: "The true starting point of history is always some present situation with its problems" and "local or home geography is the natural starting point" (Dewey, 1916/1966, pp. 214, 212). It will be evident how this idea leads directly to a radically different curriculum from the recapitulationist idea.

Dewey's concern with the psychology of the child, making the curriculum material accommodate to that rather than the other way around, provided the defining characteristic of progressivism. A further refinement of this basis of progressivism has grown out of the work of Jean Piaget. One of Piaget's crucial insights came during his work with Binet, constructing early intelligence tests. Piaget became interested in the patterns of incorrect answers commonly given to certain questions. From this, and then close observation of his own children's development, and a gift for theorizing, came his theory of intellectual development. This provided additional support to Dewey's more informal observations, and led to the now dominant sense of children's minds as not unresisting *tabular rasa*, but as active and, further, as highly structured. Rather than children's minds being structured by the logic of whatever content was impressed into them, Piaget's influential view represents the child's ability to learn as subordinate to the developing structures of their minds.

The combination of Dewey's and Piaget's influence, and, of course, the perversions, degenerations, elaborations, and simplifications their ideas have undergone in educational

literature, provide the main sources of support for the *ad hoc*
principles criticized in the first chapter. The "expanding
horizons" curriculum structure, most evident in social studies
but influential in all areas, is one of the most visible im-
plementations of those *ad hoc* principles.

Dewey's "psychological method," and principles such as
"the known to the unknown," tend to conflict with the
recapitulationist idea. If we must start with the local,
familiar, and the present we can only reach early epochs
much later when we have expanded our local concepts adequately. This, it was assumed, must take years. Also, it was
argued especially by "social efficiency" progressivists, what
most mattered was that children dealt with the twentieth
century reality around them. It was the influence of these
principles that killed off recapitulationism in North America
by the nineteen twenties.

Clearly nothing I have written in previous chapters is in
conflict with the idea that children's minds are active and that
children's distinctive ways of making sense of the world need
to be attended to in designing a curriculum. To the degree
that we accept this idea, we are influenced by the basic insights of progressivism. Even those of us who regret what appear to be simplistic extrapolations from Piaget's theory to
education must acknowledge that our sensitivity to children's
distinctive ways of making sense of the world owe much to
Piaget. So while I am proposing principles that directly conflict with some of the dominant Deweyian/Piagetian principles, it is proper to acknowlege that at some level their insights have been extremely important and influential even on
those of us who may seem to be opponents of some of their
particular proposals.

The alternative principles outlined in the first two
chapters seem to lead to a distinct idea for the organization of
the curriculum. Having undermined the principles on which
the expanding horizons form of curriculum rests we are freed
from the constraint of believing that new knowledge cannot
be meaningfully introduced except by some content associa-
tion with knowledge gained from the child's present experience. The key point in this alternative is that new
knowledge be organized in terms of the basic, usually binary,

conceptual tools which children already have in place. This means that any knowledge that can be organized in such terms can be made meaningful and can be introduced into the elementary curriculum. The criteria that will determine our curriculum content, then, will be different from the psychological criteria that have been so prominent in Dewey's progressivism and in the Piagetian influenced neo-progressivism. If we are to reduce our reliance on these criteria, with what are we to replace them?

One very general criterion follows from the replacement of the expanding horizons principles by the story-form model principles. These imply that the content of the curriculum, to be of maximum educational value, needs to reflect the power and fundamental importance of the conceptual tools it is to be built upon. By the time they arrive in school, children have been dealing with, and have developed the concepts to deal with, matters of love and hate, good and bad, fear and courage, confidence and anxiety, and so on. Their experience of the world has been dramatic and significant. For maximum educational value, we need to present the most dramatic and significant features of the world and human experience to them.

The result of the *ad hoc* principles, though this was far from Dewey's intention, has been to influence the curriculum to present to the child the superficial trivia of their local world. The alternative principles do not require that we brutalize or terrorize children with all the horror and awfulness of human experience and history, but rather that we do present human experience in a manner that does not trivialize it, bowdlerize it, or sentimentalize it. The alternative principles require that we respect children's intelligence and appreciate more fully that by age five they already have in place the most important and powerful tools that can be used to make sense of the most important and powerful knowledge about the world and experience.

The general criterion, then, is — not coincidentally — the same that provides the starting question in the alternative model: What is important? By itself, of course, this does not take us far enough to structure a curriculum — though it does provide a guiding criterion for our selection of content.

The alternative principles lead us further, and in the direction that has already given us our model, and title. They suggest that we see the curriculum as a whole as the great story we have to tell to our children.

As "primitive" tribes tell their children the myths of the tribes, so we might think of the curriculum as the lore of our complex tribe. The myths of the tribe encoded all that was most true and significant. Thinking of it this way will encourage us to focus on making the curriculum a coherent narrative of the most true and significant aspects of the world and experience. How might we do this?

AN OVERALL STRUCTURE

I have argued that in our elementary school we must make matters of human importance central, that children can have access to these, that their access is largely by means of powerful binary opposite concepts, and that the story form is a dominant sense-making tool. These principles lead to an elementary curriculum which might be labeled a Great True Stories of the World curriculum.

That is, the early curriculum would be designed to introduce children to the great stories by which we can make sense of our world and experience. Again, to emphasize, these are not fictional stories. These are the stories of science, technology, language, history, life on earth, the stars and planets, and so on. History, for example, can be made accessible as the great stories of the struggle for freedom against tyranny, for security against arbitrary violence, for knowledge against ignorance, and so on. The content of the history curriculum for the early years, then, will be made up from such powerful themes, shown through the most vivid and dramatic historical material. This will involve neither falsifying nor bowdlerizing history. It will involve simplification, but even the most sophisticated historical account involves simplification.

The science curriculum would be made up of what we know about the stories of life on earth, of our place in the universe, and of the human ingenuity which discovered the material for these stories. That ingenuity would be seen also in the stories of technological accomplishments, such as the story of our building machines to fly, from Daedalus to space-ships, of making and manipulating symbols, from the beginnings of alphabets, syllaberies, and numbers to the book and the computer, and so on.

One of the greatest of human stories is that of the elaborate creation of images that have no evident purpose; that activity we call art. The meaning of this story can only be conveyed as children are engaged in it. One can tell an historical story that engages the child's active concepts of fear and courage, but the story of art can become meaningful only as we help the child see the ways in which our actions can express and make public some undefinable thing within us. The expressive arts of music, painting, making images, controlled physical movement, and so on, are central to a Great Stories of the World curriculum, simply because they represent perhaps the greatest of our stories. In the face of all the horror, the small-minded stupidity, the endless bloody wars, and inevitable death, people have gone on and on constructing things of beauty. A curriculum that sees the arts merely as "frills" is not educational.

In the Great Stories of the World curriculum, then, teachers can be seen as the story-tellers of our tribe. My aim here is no more than to indicate that the principles outlined earlier have implications for the curriculum as well as for teaching. Not surprisingly perhaps we find a common element at the core of each, that of the story form. As teachers are our professional story-tellers, so the curriculum is the story they are to tell. The art of teaching is, in this view, tied to the ancient and powerful tradition of story-telling.

CONCLUSION

This amounts to no more than a hint in the direction of the kind of curriculum the story-derived principles lead us towards. It is, however, a hint that any of us can follow, and try to elaborate into a more rounded curriculum. What is I think clear is that the principles outlined earlier do lead to a distinctive and coherent curriculum for the elementary school.

This Great Stories curriculum is derived, hardly surprisingly nor by any complicated series of inferences, from the simple observations about children's imaginative activity with which the book began. These in turn were connected with the story form as one of our main tools for making sense of the world. None of this involved sophisticated psychological theorizing nor epistemological analysis. We are accustomed to educational implications being derived from psychological theorizing and epistemological analysis, even though many practitioners remain uncomfortable with many of these implications. Where do these story-centred criteria fit in the story of recent curriculum development?

A common story-line used to make sense of the recent history of curriculum development sees a general progression from a focus on content and its logical structures, to a focus on social relevance, to a focus on a developmental view of the child and learning. This story intersects closely with the earlier one about the dominant ideas affecting the overall structure of the curriculum. Fitting them together would be possible if we see the recapitulationist idea as a preliminary step towards developmentalism and seeing the Deweyan and Piagetian forms of progressivism as representing respectively an emphasis on social relevance and then on developmentalism. (It might be noted that the recapitulationist notion of developmentalism was in some ways more educationally useful than the more restricted psychological developmentalism of recent times; it dealt not just with the individual but with the individual in a complex cultural process.)

On the whole, this is not so much a neat sequential story in which the later phase replaces whatever preceded it. Rather we find that the later phase enjoys a fashionable dominance in the literature of education, but in practice does not replace but rather compromises with the earlier phases. Modern practice, then, is more like a coalescence of these major focuses, or a palimpsest, with varying degrees of influence exerted by each in individual teachers' classrooms. The rise of progressivism, for example, did not displace the logical concerns with content. Progressivism, as Dewey argued, tried to draw attention to the individual child's ways of learning. Unfortunately, rather than seeing simply an additional layer of sensitivity introduced, we found instead fights between those who considered content a more important focus than children's learning, or vice versa — yielding mindless and entirely unhelpful slogans such as "We teach children not subjects," and similar counter-slogans from the other side.

The dominant focus taken — whether content, society, or the individual child — tends to lead to different kinds of curricula, and different overall curriculum structures. Thus, put very crudely, the dominance of a focus on content tends to yield a curriculum divided into distinct disciplines; the dominance of a focus on society tends to lead to an interdisciplinary organization focused on issues considered relevant to the social experience of children; the dominance of individual development tends towards integrated studies, because the focus on the development of intellectual skills tends to suppress the importance of content and its distinct forms. (Piagetians, for example, stress that "the *spontaneously* growing intelligence of the child should be the focus of grade-school activities and that all else should be subordinated to this priority" (Furth, 1970, p. ix), or that the purpose of educational institutions is "to lead children towards intellectual development" (Renner, 1976, p. 4), or as Piaget himself puts it "The ideal of education is not to teach the maximum, to maximize the results, but above all to learn to learn, to learn to develop, and to learn to continue to develop after leaving school" (Piaget, 1973, p. 30).)

These foci, too, tend to favor particular forms of educational research. The content focus tends to be the domain of philosophy of education, the social focus that of sociology of education, and the developmental focus that of pyschology of education. This is too slick, of course, but not fundamentally wrong, I think. The varying foci of the different research communities in education — communities whose fortunes seem to rise and fall with the shifting dominance of content, society, and child — tend to have led to segmenting research on education. Again crudely, philosophers have tended to focus on the logic and structures of content, sociologists on matters of social relevance, and psychologists on matters of learning and development — all yielding implications to educational practice. The overall idea is that these should complement each other, but in fact we rarely see cooperation of this kind. Rather there seems to be mutual incomprehension and more or less subdued hostility among them. Even though we are now predominantly in — or perhaps moving out of — the developmentalist phase, the sociologists and philosophers continue to press the significance of the implications for the curriculum that seem to follow from their studies.

The common text-book exhortation that follows the laying out of this story-line is that we should seek for balance among the implications that follow from focusing on content, or on society, or on the child. Where then does the Great Stories of the World curriculum fit into this story? Is it derived from logical, sociological, psychological, or some other logical principles? Is it an expression of a balanced view over these fields of study? It seems to me that the Great Stories curriculum is not derived from or dependent on any of these. An implication of this approach seems to me to see these various research programs as tending to so segment education that they address problems that are different from those the educator is trying to answer.

One could of course argue that this Great Stories curriculum has a sophisticated psychological base: being the inferences about the mind that are to be drawn from the study of the story form as an expression of a fundamental mental structure; or is sociologically based in the principles of relevance that determine which stories are important for making sense of present experience; or is philosophically based in the logic of the story narrative. It is no coincidence that linguistics, psychology, and philosophy have found an important meeting place in the study of narratives. But none of this makes compelling sense — feels like the right story line. I think it is not so much a balance among the research strategies developed during this century as an appeal to an older and more pervasive principle of coherence: that of the story form. It derives from an attempt to see the curriculum as a coherent whole, with a coherent purpose, rather than as the product of implications from segmented and divergent research programs. This is not to attempt to displace those research programs, of course, but to find some source of coherence which could assess and integrate their implications for the curriculum.

CONCLUSION

The image of the teacher as the teller of our myths — when "myth" is understood in its common anthropological sense of that lore which is considered most true and significant — may strike some readers as an unfortunate choice of metaphor. Indeed, it might be argued, the "primitive" myths might convey certain aspects of their social reality in story form, and even include knowledge about their economic life, their agricultural practices, and so on. But in addition, the young of the tribe have to master the practical skills of their daily life. In the case of our more complex society these practical skills are much more pervasively required, and our schooling needs to be commensurately more concerned with such things.

I hope this is not seen as an adequate argument against my proposal; as though I am arguing for stories and against skills. I have of course stressed throughout the use of the story, the game, the joke in planning the teaching of almost everything, including basic skills. My concern is with the coherence of what is taught and with its making sense to children. In the context of a Great Stories curriculum, and in using the story-form model in planning, we have, I think, some useful tools for ensuring better educational experiences for the bulk of elementary school children. The story shapes the world's meanings for us willy-nilly. We might sensibly use its power to communicate with children more effectively.

There are two further possible objections that I should address. First, however persuasive some teachers might find my argument, there remains what may seem an insurmountable practical obstacle. It is just too difficult for the busy teacher to plan lessons according to the story-form model. Two things need to be borne in mind with regard to this obstacle. Normally, once the teacher is familiar with the model, lessons will not need to be laid out extensively in the manner of Chapter Four. No doubt to see what are, after all, merely sketches of lessons and units spread over pages and pages is somewhat daunting. But if teachers were to photocopy page 41 of this book, which contains the sections of the model, they could use it for putting in notes for a lesson. Or a set of sheets, with a sheet for each section, might serve for planning a unit. But in addition I should point out that quite the opposite is true: the busy teacher will find this model a much easier, more natural way, of organizing lessons and units after a bit of practice. This is a claim that I can hardly establish here. And it may seem implausible. We forget perhaps how we have adapted to, and accepted, other methods of planning; how use of the objectives model, for example, has come to seem so obvious, despite its artificiality. In workshops with teachers, after taking topics at random for fifteen minutes or half an hour, and using the categories of the model to organize them, it usually becomes clear how simple and natural it is to find binary opposites and build from them a basic plot for one's lesson or unit. I must leave that as an unsupported claim here, but invite readers to experiment for themselves.

The second objection is that the curriculum and the kind of material the model constantly calls for is not readily available. There is indeed a wealth of support materials, but it is not organized in a manner to support such a curriculum in text-books. This is true, and a very real problem. But it is not, I hope, for anyone who is persuaded of the validity of this approach, an adequate reason to ignore the principles on which it is based. Individual teachers can gather what materials they can find — and there are of course many useful sources available. The only real lack at the moment are basic support textbooks. We do not have mathematics texts rich in incident, anecdote, biography, games, puzzles, stories, magic, tricks, and so on. And indeed for this model to become very widely useful such texts will have to be written. If the principles are found to be valid and the model effective, then no doubt such texts will quickly become available.

Perhaps I should conclude by making clear that what I have tried to do in this book is not invent some entirely original system which teachers ought now to begin following. Rather I see this model as a systematization of what good teachers already do. My contribution is not any insight into planning teaching but rather finding categories for what I have observed successful teachers doing. Sometimes they will say "I don't know why the lesson(s) on x goes on so well. I even have kids refer to it years later." When we analyse such lessons or units in detail, we find the elements that I have tried to build into the story-form model. What is usually most educationally effective is telling children good stories about their world and about the variety of human experience in it.

* * * * *

It is very easy to let the elaboration of an idea carry one further than initially intended. I think I have been guilty of this. The spirit in which I started the book was to offer the story-form model as a supplement or alternative to the dominant model — not as a replacement for it! My intention was to design a model that brought to central prominence a number of things that I thought tended to be neglected in the dominant model. I have perhaps inadvertently shown the power of binary opposites by occasionally setting up my alternative as though in direct opposition to Tyler's object-ives — content — methods — evaluation scheme. While there are of course areas where their underlying principles come into conflict, it would be silly to suggest that they are mutually exclusive approaches. My enthusiasm for this alternative model occasionally may have led me to see binary opposites and story forms everywhere, perhaps even where other structuring forms would have been more appropriate. This is not to withdraw any of my arguments for the value and uses of the model, so much as to suggest a more balanced view of its applicability.

Teachers who might find the story-form model appealing will, of course, make their own decisions about how, where, and to what degree they will use it. No doubt many will want to integrate some aspects of it with an objectives-model. One teacher, whose work I greatly respect, has said that she finds it better to use the traditional objectives model for the overall design of units, and finds the story-form model better for planning individual lessons within that overall design. Perhaps some teachers might find they work comfortably with them the other way around.

Anyway I would like to finish at least in the same spirit in which I began; offering this as an alternative model that might be used to supplement the virtues of the dominant model. I hope teachers will take the model, and tinker with it to make whatever parts of it they find useful work best for them.

I have tried also to sketch and support as well as I can some of the principles on which the model is based. These principles seem to me sound, and they also seem to point towards an alternative and distinctive curriculum.

REFERENCES

Callahan, Raymond E. (1962). *Education and the Cult of Efficiency.* Chicago: University of Chicago Press.

Dantzig, Tobias. (1967). *Number: The Language of Science.* New York: Free Press. (New York: Macmillan, 1930).

Dewey, John. (1916/1966). *Democracy and Education.* New York: Free Press.

Dewey, John. (1958). *Philosophy of Education.* Patterson, NH: Littlefield, Adams.

Dodge, Richard Elwood and Kirchwey, Clara B. (1901). "The Course in Geography in the Horace Mann Schools." *Teachers College Record, 2* (2), 63-80.

Donaldson, Margaret. (1978). *Children's Minds.* London: Croom Helm.

Egan, Kieran. (1979/1985). *Educational Development.* New York: Oxford University Press. Revised version: *Individual Development and the Curriculum.* London: Hutchinson.

Egan, Kieran. (1983a). "Social studies and the erosion of education." *Curriculum Inquiry, 13,* 195-214.

Egan, Kieran. (1983b). "Educating and socializing: A proper distinction?" *Teachers College Record, 85*(1), 27-42.

Egan, Kieran. (1983/1984). *Education and Psychology: Plato, Piaget, and Scientific Psychology.* New York: Teachers College Press. London: Methuen.

Egan, Kieran. (In press). *Education and Modern Consciousness.* Vol. I: *Primary Understanding;* Vol. II: *Romantic Understanding.*

Eisner, Elliot W. (1978). "What do children learn when they paint?" *Art Education, 31*(3), 6-10.

Elkind, David. (1984). "Education for educators."*Contemporary Psychology, 29*(8), 644-645.

Furth, Hans G. (1970). *Piaget for Teachers.* New Jersey: Prentice-Hall.

Gatewood, C.W. & E.S. Osbourn. (1963, December). "Improving science education in the United States." *Journal of Research in Science Teaching, 1,* 355-399.

Hallam, R.N. (1966). *An investigation into some aspects of historical thinking of children and adolescents.* M.Ed. Dissertation, Leeds University.

Hallam, R.N. (1975). *A study of the effect of teaching method and the growth of logical thought with special reference to the teaching of history.* Ph.D. Thesis, Leeds University.

Hayek, F.A. (1969). "The primacy of the abstract." In Arthur Koestler and J.R. Smythies (Eds.), *Beyond Reductionism.* New York: Macmillan.

Hughes, Ted. (1977, September). "Myth and education." *Times Literacy Supplement,* 11-13.

Kehoe, John. (1984). *Achieving Cultural Diversity in Canadian Schools.* Cornwall, Ontario: Vesta Publications.

Kendall, Janet Ross. (1985). "Read to your students every day." *Reading-Canada-Lecture, 3*(3), 234-237.

Lévi-Strauss, C. (1966). *The Savage Mind.* Chicago: University of Chicago Press.

Miller, Jonathan. (1978). *The Body in Question.* New York: Random House.

Nyberg, David & Egan, Kieran. (1981). *The Erosion of Education: Socialization and the Schools.* New York: Teachers College Press.

Piaget, Jean. (1951). Plays, Dreams and Imitation in Childhood. New York: Norton.

Piaget, Jean. (1973). *The Child and Reality* (Arnold Rosin, Trans.). New York: Grossman.

Renner, John W. (1976). In John W. Renner et al. (Eds.), *Research, Teaching and Learning with the Piaget Model.* Norman, Oklahoma: University of Oklahoma Press.

Stein, Nancy & Trabasso, Tom. (1982). "What's in a story: An approach to comprehension and instruction." In R. Glaser (Ed.), *Advances in Instructional Psychology.* Vol. 2, Hillsdale, N.J.: Erlbaum.

Tyler, R. (1949). *Basic Principles of Curriculum and Instruction.* Chicago: University of Chicago Press.

Wadsworth, Barry J. (1978). *Piaget for the Classroom Teacher.* New York: Longman.

Whitehead, A.N. (1929). *The Aims of Education.* New York: Macmillan.

INDEX